Against Principalities and Powers

D0611083

ORBIS  BOOKS

Maryknoll, New York 10545

AGAINST PRINCIPALITIES AND POWERS

LETTERS FROM A BRAZILIAN JAIL

Carlos Alberto Libanio Christo

Translated by John Drury

Originally published in 1971 as *Dai sotterranei della storia*

Second Edition, enlarged, 1973

Copyright © 1971 by Arnoldo Mondadori Editore, Milan, Italy

English translation copyright © 1977 by Orbis Books

Orbis Books, Maryknoll, New York 10545

Printed in the United States of America

Library of Congress Cataloging in Publication Data

Christo, Carlos Alberto Libanio, 1944–
    Against principalities and powers.

    Translation of Dai sotterranei della storia.
    Includes index.
    1.   Political prisoners—Brazil—Correspondence.
2.   Christo, Carlos Alberto Libanio, 1944–
I.   Title.
HV9593.C45513   365'.45'0924 [B]   76-43030
ISBN 0-88344-007-5
ISBN 0-88344-008-3 pbk.

We are contending against principalities and powers,
against the world rulers of this present darkness.
Therefore take the whole armor of God,
that you may be able to withstand in the evil day,
and having done all, to stand.

Ephesians 6:12–13

Contents

Foreword ix

Abbreviations xiii

Letters from Prison
    1969 1

    1970 13

    1971 139

    1972 205

    1973 221

A Prisoner's Prayer 227

Epilogue 229

Notes 231

Index 237

Foreword

The letters collected in this volume were written by Carlos Alberto ("Betto") Libanio Christo, theology student, member of the Dominican order, and formerly director of Student Catholic Action. After twenty-two months in prison awaiting trial, he was charged with participation in subversive acts and projects and sentenced to four years on September 14, 1971.

The letters need no commentary. Here I should simply like to recount some of the events leading up to Betto's imprisonment.

Carlos Alberto Libanio Christo was born in Belo Horizonte on August 25, 1944, into a middle-class traditional family from Minas Gerais, which is politically one of the most conservative states in Brazil. In Minas Gerais there began in March 1964 the movement that culminated in the military takeover of the Brazilian government. Upon completing secondary school, Betto moved to Rio de Janeiro. There he served as national director of the JEC,[1] the Young Christian Students movement, in its early efforts to infuse new life and Christian commitment into Catholic Action. In this work he collaborated with Bishop Candido Padim, who had early recognized the historical import of the new aspirations arising among Christian university students and teachers. Even then, in the early sixties, when most people still believed in the myth of "development," people in university circles were already exploring new and different ways to transform underdeveloped societies.[2] Betto enrolled in the school of journalism at the University of Rio de Janeiro, but he left the university in 1965 to enter the Dominican order. After his novitiate in Belo Horizonte, he took his first vows and then was sent to São Paulo in order to study philosophy. At the same time, he continued to take courses in communications and worked on the daily newspaper, *Folha de São Paulo*, to which he contributed articles on church renewal that proved exceedingly popular. In 1968 he made his solemn profession of vows, dedicating himself wholly to the religious life, and was sent to the state of Rio Grande do Sul to pursue his studies in theology at São Leopoldo Seminary.

There, on November 9, 1969, he was arrested by the Security Police on the charge that he had aided and abetted fugitive terrorists in crossing Brazil's southern frontier. In reality his arrest was part of a much wider campaign directed against the whole Dominican order in Brazil by the antiterrorist division of the special police services. On November 4, 1969, Carlos Marighella, the already legendary head of the ALN (Alliance for National Liberation), had been caught in a police ambush in the streets of São Paulo. Two Dominican religious were suspected of working with him, although their exact role is even now unclear. But it was enough to evoke broadcast accusations from the repressive police forces. In announcing that they had broken up a network of armed opposition, they claimed to have discovered working relationships between various guerrilla groups and members of the Dominican order. Nationwide arrests followed, from São Paulo to Rio Grande do Sul, where six priests and several dozen seminarians, including Betto, were arrested and imprisoned. Immediately the regime mounted an all-out propaganda campaign against these "terrorists." A nationwide investigation resulted in accusations against eleven Dominicans, two secular priests, and one Jesuit. The charge was involvement with the ALN "under the leadership of Carlos Marighella, carrying out administrative duties that offered aid and logistical support."

These charges furnished the excuse for an extensive campaign of vilification directed against the "progressive" wing of the church. Politically conservative factions urged the national episcopate to condemn "subversive" priests and bishops. The reaction of the hierarchy was at first ambiguous, but then Bishop Avelar Brandão, president of the Latin American Episcopal Conference, replying in the press, called the campaign a "premeditated plan to disparage the church," and his charge was picked up and repeated by the bishops of the Northeast. On November 19 the leaders of the Dominican order issued their own communiqué, which explicitly recognized "the sincerity of evangelical sentiment and the authenticity of love for their fellow human beings" of the imprisoned religious. Fourteen French Dominicans appealed directly to the Papal Commission on Justice and Peace, denouncing all statements that had been illegally extorted from the prisoners and emphasizing that the "Dominican Affair" could not be viewed separately from the fate of all Christians in Brazil who actively opposed government by oppression.[3]

All these statements, coming from people of widely differing outlooks, had one point in common: They appealed to the courts of justice. But in extraordinary circumstances such appeals are fruitless. Betto spent twenty-two months in prison *before* being sentenced, on September 14, 1971, to four more years in prison "without his guilt having been proven." This was the comment of Father Domingos Maia Leite, Provincial of the Dominican order in Brazil, to the press on hearing the sentence.

In prison Betto continued his theological studies, hoping ultimately to be ordained to the priesthood.

The gathering of the letters and their distribution in cyclostyle form was originally undertaken by Betto's parents. In their foreword to the letters, dated February 9, 1971, they wrote:

> We offer this selection of letters to those who are not familiar with the things he has written to us and to his friends. To follow his thinking through these letters is to discover who he is. He is here fully, for here one can see the motives and passions that guide him: love for others, a passion for justice, respect for human dignity, fidelity to the values which God entrusted to humankind so that we might prove worthy to perform the work of creation. Parents of this son whom we love and of whom we are proud, we believe that nothing more is needed to make him known to the reader acquainted with them. These letters tell you who and what he is, and they are enough to console us for the tremendous injustice he now suffers because of his love for the church.

The Italian version of these letters was based upon one of the cyclostyle sets, collated wherever possible with the original manuscript. For the safety of the persons involved, the names of the addressees have been omitted in many instances; but names of family members are given. Where the reader finds (. . .) in the text, a passage has been omitted because it concerns the author's private affairs or because it might bring harm upon another person. In a few places the hand of the prison censor has been indicated. Needless to say, all the letters passed through the hands of the prison censor.

For obvious reasons, Betto himself has not had any contact with the publisher or editor of this book. He does not know how the letters have been arranged, he has not seen the proofs, and he is in no way responsible for their publication in book form.

LINDA BIMBI

In the English edition we have numbered the letters, and an index of major themes has been added at the end of the book. Thus readers may follow Betto chronologically through his years in prison by reading the text straight through, or they can discover Betto's views on a particular subject by consulting the Index. When a letter is addressed to the same person as the letter immediately preceding, the name of the addressee is not repeated.

Special thanks are extended to Naomi Noble Richard for her assistance in the preparation of the English translation.

Abbreviations

ALN   Alliance for National Liberation. Organization based on the Cuban model, established in 1967 under the command of Carlos Marighella.

CELAM   Latin American Episcopal Conference.

CICOP   Catholic Inter-American Cooperation Program.

DOPS   Department for Political and Social Order. There is a branch in each state of the Brazilian Federation.

FAB   Brazilian Air Force

IAPI   Social Welfare Institute (Brazil).

JEC   *Juventude Estudiantil Catolica.* Catholic student movement open to students below university level.

JUC   *Juventude Universitaria Catolica.* Catholic student movement for university students.

NASA   National Aeronautics and Space Administration (United States).

NATO   North Atlantic Treaty Organization.

UNE   National Students' Union (Brazil).

VPR   People's Revolutionary Vanguard. A splinter group of the Brazilian Communist Party, commanded by Captain Lercaro.

1969

1

To Virgilio, a fellow seminarian
(shortly after Betto's arrest)

Porto Alegre
November 15

(. . .) The Holy Spirit blows where and when he wills. I'm deeply touched by your kindness and generosity, and I thank you and your friends. I remain united with you all in faith and joy.

"How blest are those who have suffered persecution for the cause of right." I embrace you warmly.

2

Porto Alegre
November 16

(. . .) Alleluia. Read John 15:18–22 and 16:1–4, the reading in today's Mass. It has been the subject of my meditation today.[4]

3

To a group of young Christians
in Porto Alegre

Porto Alegre
November 17

My dear friends, nothing new has happened here. We spend our time reading, praying, and dealing with little details that acquire great importance when you are in prison. It's like the life of a Carmelite. I have my Office here and try to pray the various Hours. I pray our heavenly Father that all this will have some meaning for the manifestation of his kingdom.

Come when you can. Everything suggests that I'll be here for a bit. I embrace you all. Let us remain united in the faith and joy of the Lord.

4

Porto Alegre
November 18

Dear Friends, thanks for everything you have done for me. I've just gotten out in the sunshine for a while. It was a fine change of scenery. (. . .) Yesterday evening we celebrated Mass here in prison. It was all very simple: Jesus here with us, our comforter and liberator.

Right now I don't need anything except the things I asked for in my note. (. . .) Please get in touch with my parents, Antonio Carlos and Stella, rua Padre Odorico 162, Belo Horizonte, telephone 22-0799.

Let us remain united in the joy of the Lord. I am here to carry out his will. Everything is grace.

I embrace you in friendship and gratitude.

5

To Virgilio

Porto Alegre
November 21

(. . .) We are well in the profound joy of the Spirit. We are grateful to be allowed to re-enact in our own lives Jesus' way to redemption. He was persecuted, imprisoned, and condemned. Shouldn't a Christian imitate his Master? We fear nothing. Jesus was calumniated, threatened, and betrayed by one of the Twelve. We are free because our freedom comes from within and no one can take it from us.

Pray for us and for the church because a new hour may well be here, the hour of "the church in prison."

In the joy of faith and the Resurrection.

6

To his sister Teresa

DOPS, Porto Alegre
November 25

Dear Teresa, this is my first letter to you from prison. I have been here for two weeks now, and I probably will be here for a long time to come. I have committed no crimes. My crime was to try to be a Christian in the true sense of the word. My crime was not to accept injustice, not to stoop to compromise with privilege. My crime was to help those who are in trouble risking their lives.

I'm not afraid. I have no regrets. I spend my days reading, thinking, and dedicating myself more to prayer. I live in complete inner freedom, content to believe that I am sharing in the mystery of Jesus Christ who was persecuted, imprisoned, and condemned for the sake of our freedom.

Time will make everything clear. I hope you all are well. (. . .)

7

To his parents

São Paulo
November 27

Dearest Mom and Dad, look beyond the factual details of what has happened. Disregard the reports and conjecture in the

5

press. Disregard the accusations against me. Only one thing is important right now: I am in jail, and it is a source of joy to me. As the Bible tells us, what is wisdom in the eyes of human beings is folly in the eyes of God, and what is wisdom in the eyes of God is folly in the eyes of human beings. My arrest should cause you no shame but pride, as it does me. I am content. My conscience is at peace because what I said and did was in the interest of a more just world and a freer earth. With so much injustice around us it's not surprising that I find myself here.

I have not felt one moment of discouragement in prison. In fact I find it a truly enriching experience. Here you learn many things and become more of a realist. In particular you discover that a person is not judged by what he does in the sight of others but by what he is within himself. I am convinced that freedom of movement is not the whole meaning of human freedom. There are cloistered monks who are completely free, and no one is free who has not yet encountered himself. Prison makes possible this encounter with oneself and with others. It leads us to explore the infinite riches of the mind and spirit.

In Porto Alegre they decreed preventive detention for me, but I learned that the trial will take place in São Paulo. Everything indicates that the whole matter will be concluded rather quickly, the president of the Republic being among those who want it that way. Our lawyer here is Mario Simas, whom I met briefly at DOPS headquarters.

I believe that my visiting hours are from one to four o'clock on Wednesday afternoons. Anyone outside my immediate family who wishes to visit me must get a permit from Judge Nelson of the Second Military Court. I'm told that no formalities are required to obtain the permit.

As for letters, please write as often as you wish and can. Thanks for the hippy shorts. Shorts are our usual dress here.

Here in prison I met Doctor Madeira, who treated me when I had hepatitis. He's been in prison for ten months and is now the prison doctor, in fact if not by official decree. He's a marvelous person.

6

I embrace the two of you and all our friends. Let us remain united in prayer that God's will, not ours, be done.

A big hug to everyone, with much trust and affection.

8

(. . .) The only news here is my new prison life. Since I only arrived here a week ago, everything is still new to me. It's likely that I will be in Tiradentes Prison for some time.[5] There are about two hundred of us political prisoners here, young people of both sexes. Our cell is big, roomy, and airy. We have two bathrooms with showers, a washtub, and a kitchen with stoves. There are thirty-two people in our cell, almost all of them young. The few older men have adapted perfectly to their new style of life. We have two injured people. One was beaten up by the police when they seized him; the other threw himself out of a fourth-floor apartment window. Both are convalescing now. The group is divided into teams, which take daily turns at housekeeping. Yesterday it was my team's turn. We got up early, swept the cell, and made coffee (with milk and bread and butter). Some members of our team helped bathe the injured, while others did the cooking. I was a cook and by some miracle did not do too badly.

Occupations: French lessons, gymnastics, yoga, theology, conversations. When you have a strong spirit, prison life is tolerable. No one here seems to be unnerved or beaten down. Everyone is taking it in stride. The interrogations are finished, thank God. Now we must make the best possible use of our time here. I do not consider this time in prison a hiatus in my life. It is the normal continuation of it, and I feel keenly that I am going through a great experience (. . .).

9

Tiradentes Prison
December 13

Dear Family, Teresa has passed on to me the marvelous letter that you wrote me. It was a great source of encouragement in this difficult period. I am particularly touched by the fact that you have faced up so admirably to the ordeal of my imprisonment.

Yesterday, after I was formally sentenced to preventive detention, I was transferred from DOPS to this penitentiary. So I'm now reunited with the other Dominicans who were arrested. We are together with six other young men in a special cell. It is roomy enough, and we are a real community. We share everything we have and everything we receive. There is a stove in the cell, and we do our own cooking. A different group prepares the meals each day. I can assure you that the meals are delicious and varied.

I was at DOPS for two weeks. The first week was taken up mostly with interrogations, some of which were lengthy and exhausting. After some time and much explanation, the police were convinced that I was not so dangerous as I had been described or as the press had alleged. I am simply a Christian, and I am here precisely because I am trying to be a real one. When I realize that I belong to the church, that I, like you, am a member of Christ's mystical body, I feel proud that now I am sharing in body and spirit the situation (grace) of all those who sow the seeds of the gospel in the world. When he became man, God too was persecuted, taken into custody, tortured, and condemned to death. Paul was imprisoned for three years in Caesarea and for another two years in Rome. Peter, the leader of the apostles, was arrested in Jerusalem together with John. John was exiled to Patmos, where he wrote the book of Revelation. Stephen, James, and Simon were condemned to death in Jerusalem. In short the church to which we are joined by baptism has never been a conformist church, a rich and privileged church enjoying the favor of the powerful. It has been the church of the poor and the persecuted, the church of those who fight for justice, the church of those who act according to the Spirit rather than according to the law. Read the Acts of the Apostles. You will see that I'm right. I am very pleased that you read the Bible before meals. I will share your readings from here.

During my first week at DOPS, I was kept in solitary confinement in quite an uncomfortable cell. Then I was transferred to another cell, where I met eleven other prisoners. Most of them were young people and students. It's incredible how many university students are in prison! There were also a priest, an engineer, a dentist, a doctor, and a lawyer.

There is a great apostolic task to carry out in prison, so I do not regret being here. My only mission is to proclaim the good news of Jesus Christ. Everyone shows interest in my faith, in Christian doctrine, and in the religious life. They ask thousands of questions. It seems to me that our long chats shed some new light and help correct the distorted image many people have of Christian life and of the church.

At the same time, I am discovering here in prison young people who, though they are not religious, are living in a state of true holiness. They are pure, sincere, and wholly dedicated to their fellow human beings. They are always ready to lend a helping hand, to work for the group, and without counting the cost. I'm sure that the Spirit of God dwells in their hearts, which are full of vitality and goodness. I'm happy that God has granted me the grace to live in my own body the redemptive mystery of Jesus who, for his love of justice, was persecuted, imprisoned, and condemned to death.

Here I live with complete inner freedom. "What does it profit a man if he gains the whole world and then suffers the loss of his soul?" We used to see this gospel passage on the altar at Padre Machado,[6] if you remember.

I know that my imprisonment is a sign in the Brazilian church. I feel sure that all this is part of God's plan. Trust in him and let me play my part, just as you are admirably playing yours. He will reward us.

10

São Paulo
December 25

(. . .) We had a liturgical service with hymns and readings from the Bible. We don't celebrate Mass because the examining judge has not authorized it [censored].

I realize what this Christmas represents for our family. I'm sure that something is being born inside us, something that will bring us closer to the poor infant of Bethlehem. The Jews were waiting for a king, for the promised Messiah who would liberate Israel. Well the Messiah and king came, but without the trappings of human glory and temporal power. The authority of Jesus, the model of all authority, is that of a servant rather than a master. Christ is king because he is a servant. His birth has brought about a series of "signs of contradiction." In the life of faith no one reaches the Absolute except by passing through the insignificant.

Our family Christmas today recalls the mystery of a God who manifested himself as a poor baby in a manger. Prison is the place for evildoers, for thieves, vagrants, and criminals. It is the home of those who have been outlawed from society. Our penal system is not correctional, merely punitive. Our prisons do not reform; they corrupt and degrade. It is our honor, our glory, and our joy that our new life can be born in this "manger." But not everyone can understand this, just as not everyone can understand the mystery of the carpenter's son who suffered between two thieves. Only by the light of faith or the power of a profound ideal are such mysteries comprehensible. That is why those who have put us into prison cannot understand why we remain content, strong, and optimistic even here. We will never give them the satisfaction of seeing us sad or downcast.

I give thanks to our Father in heaven because you have grasped all this. If I have surprised you by my behavior in prison, you have surprised me much more by your capacity for understanding and affection. I am surprised, not because I expected something different, but because God has chosen our family to participate in his plan of redemption in this way. Why us and not others? Why me and not someone else? The grace in our hearts prompts us to hope that future events will prove the rightness of our way. There is no victory without a struggle (. . .).

11

To his brothers and sisters

São Paulo
December 25

(. . .) Yesterday we had visitors from noon to five o'clock. Counting the relatives and friends of the more than one hundred prisoners here, at least a thousand people must have come. Some priests came from the monastery. Teresa[7] came too, bringing cigarettes and food. The prisoners' families got to know each other. Unfortunately it rained all day, which put a bit of a damper on the visit, but despite that the prevailing mood remained festive and gay. Our pantry is now chock full. Yesterday evening we had a kind of banquet, all thirty-four of us in this cell. We had chicken, turkey, baked rice, dried fruit, and grapes. We and the prisoners in the other cells sang together. There was no wine because alcoholic beverages are not permitted, so we had to settle for tap water.

Our lawyer came to see us. He has forwarded an appeal to the Supreme Military Tribunal, requesting that we be freed on bail. I don't think the request will be considered until after the first of the year. It's certain, however, that I would not enjoy the benefits of any such grant because of the accusations against me. But there is reason to hope that our case will not drag on forever. I've heard that the president of the Republic has ordered it to be handled quickly. I myself am in no great hurry. I'll be able to pursue my theological studies in prison, so I will not be wasting any time. It's just as if I were holed up in the seminary, completely absorbed in my studies. But I enjoy an additional advantage here: I'm closer to you, and I have other Dominicans to keep me company.

A hug for all our friends and relatives. I pray for everyone, and I'm grateful to those who have stood by you in this difficult time. I wish you a happy New Year, full of peace and joy.

1970

12

To his parents

São Paulo
January 5

(. . .) Unfortunately we were not permitted to have Mass on Christmas or New Year's Day. It seems unbelievable that, in a country that calls itself Christian, prisoners cannot participate in our Lord's sacrifice. But no one can stop us from praying and thanking God for enabling us to share the experiences of his Son in our lives.

I can't tell you how happy I am to know that dad went to Holy Communion. That is the best Christmas gift our family could receive. I prayed for it many years. Now the Lord has answered our prayers. We are living a perpetual Christmas because we are being born to new life in the Spirit. I would willingly endure other prisons so that other families might know the same grace.

Last year I meditated a great deal on the mystery of the Eucharist. Jesus instituted it in his last meal with his apostles, when he told them of the sufferings he would have to endure for our redemption. He took into his hands those most ordinary of foods, bread and wine, and he consecrated them: "This is my body which will be given up for you. This is my blood which will be shed for you. Do this in memory of me." What is the meaning of these words that we repeat at every Mass? Do they simply mean that the consecration of the Mass is performed in memory of Jesus' sacrifice? No, they do not mean

15

simply that. It is true that the Mass makes his sacrifice present here and now. But it also summons us to repeat Jesus' redemptive acts so that we might truly be imitators of him. When the priest repeats Jesus' words and gestures in the Mass and says, "Do this in memory of me," I interpret it as Jesus saying to us: "I have loved you completely, so much that I willingly died for you. I have given all that I am to free you. Having nothing left but my life, I did not grudge that either. I gave it up to show you that the limits of love are to love without limits. I have given you my body and blood. I have made this gesture a sacrament so that at any time or place in human history you may receive and re-enact my life in your own. When I said, 'Do this in memory of me,' I did not mean that you should simply commemorate what I had done. I meant that you should do likewise, that you too should offer your body and blood for the redemption of humanity. Just as at Mass you receive my body and blood so in your lives you should offer up your own so that my acts may be always present in the world through you. If other human beings receive you in their lives even as you receive me in Communion, then you and I will be in communion with each other."

Unfortunately, many Christians do not realize that Mass is something to be lived rather than merely attended and that it is lived to the extent that we are willing to sacrifice ourselves for the liberation of human beings. This sacrifice is not suffering. It is *the supreme joy.* Why? Because in it we find love in all its transparency and we become *God's Sacrament in the world* (. . .).

13

To his family

January 12[8]

(. . .) Thanks for the stationery and for the notebook that we use to play our navy battle game. That's how Castro and I passed the time when the two of us were in separate cells at

DOPS headquarters. We shouted our moves to each other through the bars—"B-12," "B-8," "A-5"—and one guard thought we were speaking in code. In prison any unusual action or movement arouses suspicion. Sometimes the police are alarmed by a simple look or gesture. The other day, for example, we didn't have enough water in our cell. It was terribly hot and the cell was stifling. It was my turn in the kitchen, but I couldn't prepare anything because we had been given so little water. Suddenly the sky darkened—we don't see much of the sky here, to tell the truth. There was the rumble of thunder, and then it began to pour. We hung a little bucket on the end of a broom handle and stuck it through an opening to catch some rain water. But quickly a guard appeared at our cell to tell us to pull in the bucket, or else the guard on patrol outside might mistake it for some sort of signal and shoot it full of holes. The guards who patrol outside usually carry machine guns. They substitute ordinary rifles only on visiting days.

Last week they transferred our guards. I think they do it as a precaution, so that the guards don't become sympathetic to their prisoners. For the present, police from the larceny squad are here. The atmosphere is more oppressive, and security is stricter. But they haven't bothered us in our cells.

I did not hear the president's New Year's address, but I am waiting for the "facts." I dare not say "acts" for fear that they might be more of the kind already promulgated.[9] You're mistaken if you think that we owe our relatively decent treatment here to him. In fact we owe it to you, our families. The food they serve us here is intolerable. It is shipped here every day from the state penitentiary in huge canisters. We manage to eat decently only because our families send us food and we have a stove in our cell. We do our own cleaning up, and we get two periods of fresh air per week. I say "fresh air" rather than "sun" because we go out into the courtyard at stipulated times whether it's raining or not. The doctor who takes care of us is also a prisoner. Thus his services represent a saving for the government and an abuse of his professional status. The same holds true for the two dentists who are imprisoned here, one of whom is a university instructor. There has been a sudden interruption in their work, however, and we do not know why.

There is another more serious matter. Although we are prisoners of the Military Tribunal, people from DOPS often come and take one or another of us away for further interrogation. Those taken are kept at DOPS for days and may be tortured again, without judicial authorization and without their defense attorneys' knowledge. In short we live without any guarantees.

On the other hand there is on the books a decree passed by Café Filho[10] (number 38016, dated October 5, 1955) that spells out the criteria governing the treatment of political prisoners. This law guarantees us, among other things, recreation, visits from blood relations at any time, unobstructed delivery and posting of mail, and medical care by a private physician. None of these things has been permitted to us. We've sent an appeal to the court, asking compliance with this law. It doesn't seem to me that we have asked for much, but we have not yet received any replies nor has there been any change or improvement in the routine of prison life. I am telling you this so that you may form a more realistic picture of our situation. What is more, we are still forbidden to celebrate Mass. As a Christian, I do not want or expect special privileges in prison. In fact I can't really feel sorry for myself when I see so many fathers of families incarcerated here with no way of helping their loved ones or relieving their present misery. Many don't have the wherewithal to hire a lawyer. So here we all are, even though our guilt has not even been proven.

I believe it is useless to forward petitions to the government, which will show its true face when it passes formal judgment upon us. Read Paul's letter from prison to the Ephesians. I remain happy and at peace because I know I am here "for the growth and spread of the gospel." I pray that the Lord will make us instruments of his justice and peace.

Your letters do me a lot of good. Let us remain united in our faith and in our lives, both illuminated by the word of God.

P.S. 1: After dinner today some people from DOPS suddenly showed up to take away one of our fellow prisoners. Even though he is under the jurisdiction of the Military Tribunal, the Tribunal was not consulted. Even the prison warden did not know that one of his prisoners had been spirited away. DOPS wants to know where the prisoner's brother is. The brother is wanted for engaging in certain political activities. How would our fellow prisoner, who has been in jail for three months, know the whereabouts of his brother, who disappeared from his home about a week ago?

Our fellow prisoner got back around 5:00 P.M. His hands and the soles of his feet were swollen from whippings. His shoulders were bruised, and there were two red streaks from the cord they had wound around his neck. Doctor Madeira happened to be in our cell when the prisoner returned, and he saw it all. We immediately sent a protest to the warden, who said he would do something about it. But meanwhile the boy has been tortured.

P.S. 2: I think there is a pressing need to denounce, in the name of justice, the torture now going on in the prisons of Brazil. There are thirty-five people in our cell, and I am the only one who has not been subjected to physical torture. I have, however, been subjected to psychological torture, for I have been threatened and also forced to look on when other prisoners were being mistreated. If anyone in politics is interested in taking up this cause, we can readily provide him with relevant evidence and material. During the dictatorship of Getulio Vargas one lawyer, Sobral Pinto,[11] pleaded that political prisoners be granted the same protection we would readily give to animals. I think the same plea is very much in order today.

P.S. 3: If you have a chance, write to our friends down south and ask them to send me my things. All I really need are my books. Give my clothes to someone who can use them. It's not worth keeping them for me (. . .).

14

To Sister Rosa, a Brazilian nun

February 10

Dear Sister, I enjoyed your letter very much (. . .). The support and understanding of brothers and sisters in the faith are a great consolation. I feel that I am suffering for the sake of the gospel. The path of the church is that of its Master. As *Lumen Gentium* (no. 8) puts it, "Just as Christ carried out the work of redemption impoverished and persecuted, so the Church is called to follow the same path. . . . " Why shouldn't we joyfully choose to live out this same experience in our own flesh and spirit? Wasn't Jesus tortured and condemned to death? (. . .) I'm sure that the real consecration of my religious life is taking place in this prison. Isn't it what we prayed for many times during our novitiate, as we pondered the lives of the saints and asked God to let us be the last among human beings? (. . .)

Today, banned from society, locked up behind bars and guarded by soldiers, sharing my life with prisoners and criminals, I can feel the grandeur of this mystery. I now realize in my own flesh why the Lord chose to be poor when he came to proclaim our salvation, why he lived among sinners and accepted the accusations of the Pharisees against him.

I have no reason for sorrow or regret. I can only give thanks to God as I live through this continuing Lent and prepare for a truly great Easter. Under trees in the garden outside your school I was taught the catechism and prepared for my first Holy Communion. Today I feel sure that the simple notions of the gospel that I learned then are enough to help me live the mystery of faith and the life of charity in all simplicity. My parents and you nuns were God's instruments. Through you I came to know these truths, and now I try to live them as best I can.

Our Dominican community here in prison thanks you for your prayers. We know it is the only support on which we can truly rely. For our part we wish to be a sign and symbol of the church of the poor, the persecuted church mentioned in the Acts of the Apostles. The fact is that we Christians cannot live according to the law; we must live according to the Spirit. What is folly in the eyes of men is wisdom in the eyes of God.

A big hug for you and all the sisters in your community. The Dominican community in prison is joined to your community by grace and prayer as we joyfully await the approaching Easter season.

15

To his brother, Luiz Fernando

February 22

(. . .) I was so happy to see the photo of little Flavio.[12] I suddenly realized that I feel almost like a father to him. It is as if he were a part of me. Seeing him in good health, so happy and roly-poly and at the same time unaware of what the future holds in store, I felt strong enough to fight for him and his future. I want to participate somehow in the struggle for a better future for him. His life is much more important than mine. I am in the prime of youth, and I feel no weariness. It seems well worth the effort to live my life for the sake of the generations that will come after me. They have the right to expect a more just world, where people can regard each other as brothers and sisters and where the disgraceful thing we call prison will no longer exist.

Why do some human beings imprison other human beings, putting them behind bars as if they were wild animals? We can't answer that question unless we're willing to admit that we live in a primitive state. Though we have evolved materially, our moral and spiritual evolution has come to a standstill. We have not yet discovered the full power and richness of the human spirit. Perhaps the Eastern world perceives the spirit more clearly than we do. It's significant that all the great religions arose in the Orient. The West has only been able to produce refrigerators, cars, and missiles. We have become spare parts in the gigantic machinery of the industrial world, parts to be discarded when we jam the machinery or spoil the rhythm desired by those in power. The fact is that none of us is free in this respect. In one way or another we all are victims of this consumerist society in which economic profit is the basic objective.

There is in me a sense of justice that keeps me from accepting all this as a normal state of affairs. It is not just or right. When I look around at the world and then at the picture of Flavio, I am ashamed that I cannot offer him something better. The justification for our struggle and our sacrifice is to be found in little Flavio, in the children of my fellow prisoners here, in all the children of this country who will learn in school that we are a free nation—just because a Portuguese monarch raised the cry for independence on the bank of a little river[13] (. . .).

16

To his family

February 22

(. . .) An official of *Operaçao Bandeirantes*[14] came and took him[15] away. This happened about a week ago. Why? No one could say, not even he as they were leading him away. We expected him to be back the next day, but he didn't return. Days went by, and still he did not return. He is there, in "that place" where many of our companions have been tortured. Even the military police themselves refer to it as "hell's annex." Today we were told that he tried to commit suicide. Again they have put him to the "parrot-perch" torture[16] and electric shock. In all likelihood they tried to "suicide" him by slitting his wrists. He was then taken to the military hospital for blood transfusions, and he is now in solitary confinement. No one can get to see him or even find out what is going on.

Yesterday the apostolic nuncio, Umberto Mozzoni, came to see us. He also tried to see him but could not. Today we all are silent. Tomorrow the same thing could happen to any one of us. We enjoy no protection, no guarantees. We are like the Jews under Nazism. Times change, but evil does not. Oppression takes new names and new forms, that is all. Our silence is like that of Mary before her son. It signifies rage at this egotistical world, but it also hopes for justice and trusts that love will have its "hour" and its chance. Have confidence in us. A big hug for all.

17

To a religious community

February 22

(. . .) It is a rainy and gloomy Sunday here. Now there are fifty of us in this cell, and we are trying to make the best of it. Many are sleeping on mattresses on the ground because there is no room for more beds. The silence reflects the darkness of this gray day. It is not the silence of tranquility or inner peace; it is a kind of suffocation. So many people together and so little talk. It's as if we wanted to scream but the sound dies in our throat, and we simply keep silent and wait. For what? I don't know. No one does. Waiting is a permanent part of life in prison. It's like waiting on a railroad platform, but here there is no train and no track. Our silence is heavy-hearted like the weather. We are like people who, being provoked, bide their time and store up energy to react and counterattack later. We can feel our own impotence. No one can help us, and we ourselves can do nothing. It isn't a dead end because we have not yet given in to discouragement. Nor is it hate because we have not yet given in to despair. Perhaps it's rage—patient, silent rage at the labyrinth of absurdity before us.

What did the Jews think about in the concentration camps, knowing they would soon die in the gas chambers? Perhaps they thought about nothing, just as many of us are doing right now. Perhaps they simply waited in silence, but not for anything in particular—not for death and certainly not for some miraculous release. Perhaps they were incapable of thinking about the unthinkable or fearing the inevitable. Once people realize that nothing depends on them any longer, that their fear is no longer a symptom of resistance, then they have nothing to do but wait in silence (. . .).

18

To his brother, Luiz Fernando

February 26

(. . .) We had a cordial visit from the apostolic nuncio. We priests and religious spoke with him for about two hours. We described our plight, and it made a deep impression on him. We have no guarantees and no security. He pledged his solidarity with us and showed great interest and understanding. He told us that Paul VI knows about our situation and that the Vatican Justice and Peace Commission knows about the tortures. After our conversation he gave us a fine box of chocolates and packs of American cigarettes. He also gave us the papal blessing. We asked him to visit the other prisoners too because the church must concern itself with the plight of *all* prisoners, not just clerics and religious. The prison warden assembled all the inmates in our wing, and the nuncio spoke to them. He alluded to the torture, showing real understanding for all those who fight in the name of justice. Then he gave the papal blessing to all, "even to non-Christians because the blessing of the Holy Father never hurt anyone." We asked him to make sure that the church took an interest in the families of those political prisoners who are really poor. He promised to get in touch with *Caritas Internationalis*[17] concerning their plight.

Today Cardinal Scherer of Porto Alegre came to visit us. He brought me a hug from Mom and Dad, whom he had seen in Belo Horizonte. He visited every cell, listened to the accounts of torture, and saw C. in our cell. C. has been in a cast since September. He cannot move, and he lies in bed without medical care.

We begged the cardinal to have the church—the only institution in Brazil not controlled by the government—take action on behalf of political prisoners. The fact is that only the church can help us now, and even its range of action is limited by the civil and military authorities.

I know Tito well. He would never become so desperate that he would try to commit suicide. I'm sure they tried to "suicide" him. It has happened to many political prisoners in our great Brazil. Yesterday the nuncio tried to see him, but they wouldn't permit a visit. Tito is back in the solitary confinement that the Military Tribunal had lifted three months ago. Who is responsible for what is going on here? Some people here lived under Fascism and Nazism, and they say that the present Brazilian regime is no different insofar as mass extermination is concerned. Others lived under the New State[18] and, according to them, the present repression is on a par with the refined police tactics of Felinto Muller.[19]

Faced with such facts, we realize how justified our struggle is. Our only regret is that we have not done much more.

I myself am fine. I have begun my theological studies again, although the judge has forbidden certain books on specific themes. The prohibition against Mass remains in effect. Such a measure can be justified only by a government that is persecuting the church.

It seems almost certain that we will be shifted to Tremembe Prison in Taubate[20] around the end of March. This will make visiting even more difficult, and we get few enough visits as it is. Anyone from Belo Horizonte who wants to visit me will have to get authorization from the Military Tribunal. And they'll say: "That guy has already had too many visitors." If that happens, my would-be visitors should reply that I specifically made arrangements to see them that week, putting off other visitors for that reason, and that they have come a long way to see me, and so forth.

A Swiss newpaper has published a report on Brazil, describing the "affair" in which I am involved. One of the questions on the entrance exam for the school of journalism in São Paulo was: "Who is Padre Betto?" When I get out, I think I will apply for some important job. . . .

A big kiss to all, especially to little Flavio.

25

19

(. . .) Tito is back with us. He stays in bed or drags himself around, limping. He is recuperating from the terrible suffering he endured. He was tortured for three days: parrot-perch, electric shock, whippings, beatings. They even reached new heights of sadism, putting an electrode in his mouth. It was the intention of the army to interrogate all the Dominicans once again, because they felt our interrogators at DOPS had been in too much of a hurry. To escape the suffering they were inflicting on him and to make a public protest against such interrogation of political prisoners, Tito finally resolved to commit suicide. He had a razor blade, and he slashed the veins and arteries on the inside of his left elbow. He lost a lot of blood.

We have done all we can to get the church to issue a protest. It must take a stand on the grave situation in Brazil before it is too late. But the bishops are used to being on the defensive, and they prefer omission to risk. Maybe someone will have to die before the church will react (. . .).

Father Vincent De Couesnongle, representing the superior general of our order, came from Rome for a quick visit. He and our father provincial spent yesterday afternoon with us. They came into the cell to see Tito. De Couesnongle said that our case has had profound repercussions in Europe. Everyone is interested and asks questions about us. The superior general has received manifestations of support and solidarity from the highest church authorities in Europe. Rome's support is unqualified, even in the Secretariat of State.

The Bible shows us clearly that God speaks through events. John XXIII reminded us that we must scrutinize the "signs of the times" in order to understand and appreciate God's activity in history. I believe that the events in which we have been involved here, through no merit of our own, are due to the action of God's Spirit. God is speaking to the church of Brazil and the church of Latin America through what is happening to us. That is why I feel we have nothing to lose and why I trust in God's providence. Tito's case is a striking proof of it.

In all likelihood the final results of the investigation into our case will be handed over to the court on the tenth of this month. Then the charge will be drawn up. I ardently wish that this phase of the whole process is handled quickly. Once I know the final verdict, I will be able to plan out my life in prison a little better. I feel psychologically ready for whatever happens to me. Living here with young people whose sentences will certainly be upwards of twenty years, I feel that our case is almost laughable. They are supported only by the strength of their ideals, while I have the support of the church. Their calm is a challenge to us.

(. . .) As far as little Tony's[21] First Communion is concerned, I think it's better to educate him in the faith and then wait for him to express a desire for Communion. He shouldn't be confronted with an obligation. No one should be "prepared for First Communion" specifically, but rather formed in the Christian faith.

A big hug to you all. Let us await Easter in unity. Now is the hour of the Passion. Soon there will be light!

20

March 7

(. . .) Everything is going along fine here. Nothing new, as is usually the case in prison. Living with my fifty fellow inmates continues to be a rich and beneficial experience for me.[22] I am learning to belong more to others than to myself. Here no one claims priority or precedence. What belongs to one belongs to all. We have the whole day to listen to the radio, read, study, chat, and play bridge. But we must go to bed before one o'clock and get up before nine. I prefer to get to bed around eleven and to rise between 6:30 and 7:00, because I can organize my day better when I do. In time, you scarcely notice that you're in prison. It's as if we all had freely chosen this mode of life. The body adapts little by little, and we undergo surprising changes. After being in prison for awhile, there is nothing new to see or touch. But the sense of hearing gradually becomes more acute. We can recognize any outside noise, to the point of being able to tell the make of a car by its sound alone. We know instantly when the mess wagon has arrived and when the jailer is climbing the stairs to our cell. One sense quickens as another atrophies.

Sometimes I try to imagine what my life would be like under normal conditions. It would certainly be different now, after this experience in prison. For example, we've learned to eat everything with a spoon; we can handle it as if it were fork and knife too. Forks and knives aren't indispensable; they are a matter of habit. Nor do we need two dishes for a meal; the same plate serves for main course and dessert. We have learned to skin oranges with our hands as cleanly as if we had a knife. Till now I could never read lying down without soon getting sleepy and dropping the book. Now I can spend a whole day in bed reading without feeling the least bit sluggish. Our body adapts slowly but surely, without our noticing it. Our basic needs are reduced, and our physical resistance increases. Today I could live perfectly well with two pairs of pants and two shirts. Prison is a great education in this respect. It teaches one to live in community, to study in the midst of noise, to sleep with the light on (. . .).

21

To his brothers and sisters

March 7

(. . .) What a pleasant surprise Mom pulled on me last Wednesday! (. . .) I have already begun to celebrate Dad's birthday in my prayers. It seems to me that we have little to ask and much to be thankful for. What I love most in Dad is his youthful spirit. It is evident in his ability to grasp the new historical situation in which we are involved as agents. Having eight children requires him to have great understanding and inner serenity. He cannot permit himself a one-track mind, because each of his children has a different way of life. The important thing is that we all have the same vision of humanity and the world, a vision acquired from our upbringing. How we make that vision real, or how we struggle to make it real, depends on the opportunities that life affords each of us. When I was Leo's age,[23] I never expected to end up in prison. Today prison life is a reality of which I am proud.

(. . .) Today our case is supposed to have reached the Military Tribunal. I think we'll know something about how it's going before this month is over. There is continued support for us in Europe, as we learned from the Sunday edition of *O Estado de São Paulo*.[24] We also learned that Dad got the letter we sent him and was deeply moved.

Sunday we decided, among other things, to use up a little energy. We pushed all the beds to the back of the cell, used two beams to fashion a makeshift goal, rolled our socks into a goodsize ball, and played a game of soccer. But the ball was pretty small and the players numerous, so we had a kneeing free-for-all that left us all hobbling around for a day. I was the goalie on my team, which won despite the poor showing I made (. . .).

22

To his parents

March 8

(. . .) I simply can't understand why you haven't gotten the letter I wrote you. It must have gotten lost. I thank you for the Easter greetings and wish you the same. We are very close to each other, even though I cannot be with you in person to celebrate the feast.

(. . .) There is one less prisoner here in cell 7. Otavio Angelo (whom I lent my bed to when he arrived a month ago) is now in Mexico, freed in exchange for the Japanese consul.[25] He and Diogenes de Oliveira were in this prison.

If any of us gets around to writing his prison memoirs, the chapter on this particular stretch of confinement will be one of

29

the most interesting. We've lived through unforgettable experiences this week. Never has freedom seemed so easy or so alluring. But like in a game with many players and few winners, no one knew who would luck out.

We heard about the whole thing shortly after visiting hours on Wednesday, but we remained sceptical. The kidnappers had spirited away the consul without leaving any note in his car—as had been done, for example, in the kidnapping of the American ambassador. There was doubt and uncertainty surrounding the whole affair. Suspicion arose, voiced by the personnel of the Japanese consulate and propagated by the press, that the kidnapping might be the work of common criminals seeking a ransom. Our terrible tension, along with our hope, increased by the hour. If the kidnapping was a political protest, who would be selected for the exchange? From Wednesday to Sunday all the radios in our cell were left on, tuned to the various stations that were on the air. By Thursday the kidnappers' silence was getting on our nerves. People were chain-smoking, thinking and talking of nothing else. Finally we realized that there was nothing more for us to say, that we had exhausted every hypothesis, but we kept returning to the topic in the hope of uncovering some new angle. Thursday afternoon the radio reported that the kidnapping had been carried out to secure the release of a certain number of political prisoners in exchange for the consul. The kidnappers had surfaced.

Our cell teemed with hopeful expectation. Some of our fellow inmates, who would almost certainly be sentenced to more than twenty or thirty years in prison, were filled with a singular euphoria. They seemed transfigured as they thought of themselves free and safe outside the country. They literally quivered with the force of attraction that freedom exerts on all human beings. But we still had to find out which political organization had pulled off the kidnapping, how many names were on their list, and whose.

Many political prisoners are registered by the police as belonging to specific leftist organizations. Once the kidnappers declared who they were, we could at least begin to guess who might be on their list for the exchange. But we still didn't know what criteria the kidnappers might use or whether they would demand the release of more prisoners than had the kidnappers of the American ambassador. That same afternoon our new sense of security was greatly diminished when we learned that the communiqué had been signed by Lucena of the VPR command and that he was only asking for the release of five political prisoners. Considering the critical legal situation of numerous prisoners, his demands seemed much too modest. From the fact that he had signed the communiqué, we deduced that his wife (who was later killed in a shootout with the police) would be one of the five prisoners in question and that at least three would be released from our prison. A number of VPR militants are imprisoned here. Otavio Angelo never expected to be included in the list because he is considered a member of the ALN.

The list of names was made public Friday afternoon. Otavio turned pale with emotion when he heard his name. He had only been in prison two months. The inclusion of Mother Maurina's name[26] was a big surprise. The first wave of emotion was followed by a general outburst of sheer joy. Otavio started packing his bag, expecting them to come for him at any moment. In the meantime we all joined in singing to celebrate his freedom. The prevailing joy was reminiscent of the evening before a general amnesty. Only the weariness caused by nervous tension allowed some of us to get to sleep that night. The radios were left on because the police could not find a prisoner whose code name was listed as Toledo. There was a fresh wave of hope and a new round of conjecture.

The next morning we learned that the kidnappers had proposed a new name in place of Toledo. It was Diogenes de Oliveira, a prisoner in cell 5 of our prison.

DOPS came around two in the afternoon to pick up the freed prisoners for their plane flight out of the country. We cheered them as they left, and they were deeply moved but tried to maintain an air of serenity and dignified pride.

A list of only five names had not left us too much scope for conjecture. Before it was released to the public, we had thought it might contain the names of those who had kidnapped the American ambassador and had subsequently been arrested. Two of them are here. Working on the same supposition, the mother of one of them had rushed here to say goodbye to her son. But we were conjecturing amid an unexpected and fast-moving turn of events.

This affair may have some impact on our trial. Contrary to our expectations the report of the investigation into our case has not yet been handed in to the Military Tribunal. I personally am in no hurry. In the letter Mom wrote me last week, I noted a certain concern over the adverse effect my arrest might have on our family. I would very much like you all to look at the whole matter from my point of view, from the point of view of faith, of surrender to God's will, of service to our people and to history (. . .).

23

To a community of nuns

March 10

Dear Friends, I am writing to thank you for the support you have given my family. I also want to thank you for your prayers and for the books you sent (. . .).

It is as if the whole situation confronting us today has been revealed to us, and we suddenly realize that this is the path Jesus has chosen for his church. *Lumen Gentium* leaves no room for doubt about that. Once we sat at table with the rich, frequented stately mansions, and shared the dais of the powerful. The time has come for us to turn to the poor and the persecuted, the fighters for justice, the prisons; for it is a time of oppression. We do not regret ending up behind bars if it is important for the sake of the gospel and the church.

Here among our cellmates—political prisoners and common prisoners—we have found the living image of Jesus Christ. For us prison is truly a *theological experience.* Only by actually living it can you get some idea of the richness it offers. You come to see why the Christian's way to glory leads through the cross. It is the logic of the Servant of Yahweh. Many prisoners have read the books you sent. The stories that impress them most are those of Moses, Jesus' trials, and Demetrius.[27] But they pose an interesting question: "Why is the church only now presenting things from this viewpoint?" Our answer is closely related to our explanation of the fact that Christians are only now ending up in prison.

Every day we read the book of Psalms. The military authorities have decided that we are no longer Christians, much less religious, so they don't let us celebrate Mass here, but they cannot stop us from praying. We recite the Psalms together daily. Some of our lay companions pray with us out of the same book. One, a native of India, reads the Psalms for half an hour every morning. It reminds me of Bonhoeffer, a member of the Underground and prisoner of the Nazis, who wrote that he had found the Psalms to be the best form of prayer. *Prison is a privileged place of "metanoia" and "koinonia."* There Saint Paul was tempered, there the apostles spent some time, the martyrs and mystics, like Saint John of the Cross, turned their cells into cages of divine love.

The reason is that, in prison, life is seen as if it were a photographic negative. A developed print, which takes full advantage of the play of light, can sometimes create a false picture of reality. We sometimes need raw reality to work out the full potentiality of what is real. *Daydreams and mere fancies gradually fall away when torture confronts us with the prospect of death.* When we discover the full depth and dimension of the inner person, the outer person diminishes. We realize that life comes down to a few basic needs and a few essential values. This reduction to our basic and primeval dimensions shows us that the one and only real vocation of human beings is to take part in the intimacy of God. The more we cling tooth and nail to suffering, the closer this intimacy becomes (because we cannot evade suffering, and the only way to overcome it is to confront it with as much courage as possible). Just as sickness helps us to realize the value of good health, so prison reveals the true worth of freedom.

There is a lot of useless freedom on the outside. We are free only when we commit ourselves to the risk of history, when we decide to intervene in reality in such a way that it will be transfigured by our actions. It may well be that right now our deeds constitute a mystery for some people. But don't the purest and most authentic realities spring from mystery? There is no other way. God could not remain metaphysically suspended over us. It was inevitable that he would immerse himself in history, that in revealing himself he would reveal us—and vice versa. Dialogue presupposes encounter. Christ is a part of history at the same time that he transcends it. Here the freedom of the Christian is completed and fulfilled. The Incarnation is followed by the Resurrection.

So we must tell our companions here that we will remain "subversives" as long as one human being remains oppressed. Our commitment is not to one specific form of government, to one ideology or labor organization. Our commitment is to man, whose dignity we recognize and proclaim as forcefully as it is denied. There's no doubt that purgatory must exist as the state of tension between love and indifference in which you have no possibility of choosing between them. God chooses for us. Sometimes he even chooses against our will, as he chose for the reluctant prophets and also, I am sure, for the seven Dominicans, two secular priests, and the Jesuit who are imprisoned here. The choice has been made for us. Turning back now would not be prudence; it would be treason. Our task and duty here behind bars is clear.

Pray that all this will turn out as God wills. Pray for those prisoners who have no one on their side and who can count only on the strength of their ideals. Explain our situation to the Christian community. From the "church in prison" we send you assurances of our confidence and friendship. Now is the Passion; the Resurrection will come after.

24

To a Brazilian nun

March 10

Dearest Sister Carmen, your biscuits made a great hit here. Thanks also for the letter, which shows that our sisters in the faith are truly in communion with us. We feel the effect of their prayers. How can we explain the joy we feel, the certainty that all this is part of God's plan of salvation.

The commemoration of the Passion draws near, and as I relive in my own body the experience of Jesus Christ, I ask myself why he has chosen prison as the way. Is it not the abode of criminals and alienated people?

God chose to identify himself with the poor and the oppressed, and the religious life arose out of a need to make this same identification. People must see in us an image of their Master, and therefore we should not be afraid to follow the way of the cross. Saint Paul is a magnificent example: His apostolic journeys took him from one prison to another. Thus we learn to suffer joyfully and to die believing in life.

I believe, Sister, that we have acted according to the Spirit. I can say that without being presumptuous. We do not fear the justice of human beings because it cannot deprive us of anything, least of all the inner freedom that the Lord is now giving us.

A big hug to you and your community. Pray for us and our fellow prisoners.

Yours in expectation of the Resurrection.

25

To his parents

March 23

(. . .) Your courage in facing up to reality and your confidence in the future gives me much courage. At times, to tell you the truth, I become annoyed with myself for causing you so much anxiety. Then I realize that something else is involved here, that it has to do with the natural desire we all have to regain our freedom. But what is freedom? It is a question I frequently ask myself. There is the freedom that is based on money and the labor of others, and then there is the freedom of the human being who finds himself by giving himself, by service to others. Were the great men of history, such as Julius Caesar and Napoleon Bonaparte, free only because they did not owe obedience to anyone? Jesus Christ and Francis of Assisi chose the path of self-sacrifice, of service to others, of absolute obedience. Were they free?

In a study of freedom in the present-day world, Marcuse states that one can hardly find a free person in the United States. Yet that country is regarded as the model of freedom in the Western world. There is a high degree of social organization, resulting from the breakneck speed of a technological advance in which people are conditioned by the machine. Because of this the industrial and governmental systems strictly control the individual. The choices available to average Americans are extremely limited. They can pick a make of a car, a particular plane flight, a brand of film, or a six-pack of beer. But they have little chance to choose some alternative to the "American way of life." And despite deep-rooted religious sentiments and patterns of conduct, Americans lack spiritual depth and philosophical objectivity. They do not question or ponder their existence, much less consider changing the status quo; quite the contrary, they seek to propagate it. The results of American freedom are plainly to be seen in the newspapers: a persistent and spreading plague in Southeast Asia and the Middle East, the world's record consumption of toxic drugs, unbridled eroticism, artistic productions devoid of any constructive content (like the Hollywood productions that teach you nothing but to drink Coca-Cola), racial segregation, and so on. Such technological freedom was well analyzed and criticized by Aldous Huxley in *Brave New World*.

Even less can you talk about freedom under regimes ruled by the likes of Hitler and Stalin, where all power comes from the state and is exercised exclusively in its name, where the people are all but excluded from the political process and dissidents are imprisoned, outlawed, or killed.

The fundamental point of these examples is the fact that the state can restrict or take away freedom but can never confer it. *For freedom is something that must be won.* People must continually fight for it, even at the cost of their lives.

I believe that freedom, as a societal achievement, has not yet come into existence. So far there have been occasional moments of freedom, areas of freedom, free individuals. But freedom as a condition of life has not yet come into being. Slavery as a legal status was abolished only a century ago. But people go on creating new myths to compensate for their frustrations—new forms of subjugation, like colonialism and imperialism. The very social structure in which we live is fundamentally coercive. From the moment we come into the world we are taught what we "must not" do, we are subjected to repressive laws, and we can see a policeman on every corner. The existing social structure so exacerbates this condition that many human beings do not know what to make of freedom even when they have a chance to be free.

A century ago humankind began to discover itself through psychology, sociology, and biology. But we are still too much "outside" ourselves. We have made little use of the psychic and spiritual riches within us. I believe we will attain true freedom only when we arrive at the stage of evolution that Teilhard de Chardin calls the "noosphere," the realm of the spirit. Surely the spirit will be the last great discovery of humankind. Then we will be free because freedom will exist, first and foremost, within us.

The witness of free human beings helps us to believe in freedom and desire it. Real freedom develops inside us and radiates outward. No prison can destroy it. I have received this kind of witness from my cellmates, from children, from poets and saints, and from the poor. They are people who cannot be imprisoned by bars. They speak with their eyes, with their silences, and with their serenity. They are prophets of the spirit, who know how to lay hold of the reins of history. It is they who are really dangerous, who should be feared above all others by those who don't wish to hear the word "freedom" or admit its existence.

It's to be expected that since I'm a prisoner, I should speak of freedom. I do so because every day I discover it within myself and my cellmates and realize its value and its price (. . .).

26

To Pedro[28]

Holy Thursday

(. . .) As we see it, the causes and consequences of our imprisonment can only be analyzed in the light of God's word. By it
we can see their fullest and truest significance. In the light of
God's word we can grasp the prophetic dimension of our
"affair"[29] as it relates to the church in Latin America. This is
especially true if we consider it in dialectical terms. Indeed I
think this is the standpoint from which we should interpret the
message of creation and promise, of fall and pardon, of his-
toricity and salvation, of incarnation and resurrection, that
make up the main strands of the Bible. It seems to me that the
fundamentalist and historicist interpretations that have pre-
vailed so far are not valid. Biblical exegetes have never managed to dissociate themselves from a priori principles regarding the biblical test. They look to the Bible for a confirmation of
their own truth, not for the truths contained in revelation itself.
Or else they start from etiological and infrastructural descriptions—the more recent approach—but even this method is not
free from substantive defects. For if excessive value is placed
on just one element of the infrastructure, this can invalidate
the overall interpretation.

I readily admit my ignorance in the field of exegesis. This is
no false modesty, just an easily verifiable fact. But I'm much
inclined to take the risk of making a mistake, that is, of being
overly subjective, because I feel sure that I will know how to
correct such a mistake if necessary. Prison places us Christians
in a situation of continuing dialogue with other people of very
different tendencies from ours. A cell like this one, where fifty
people are gathered together, imposes on us a community life
quite different from the one we are used to in our religious
houses. Here there are no basic assumptions by which to
define positions or delineate the boundaries between different
faiths; and here there is no room for fear of one another. It's
confrontation and debate at every moment, and the only valid

response is our life itself. But our cellmates do have great curiosity about Christianity, and it becomes obvious that our language is inadequate to express clearly who and what we are—in contrast to their language, by the way. It is also clear that in a deeper way than us they are living certain values that we had thought were the exclusive possession of Christians raised in the theological virtues. Their appeal is strong, our response limited. For example, we are lost in astonished admiration at the witness of a young atheist here who is willing to accept martyrdom in the name of a hope rather than in the name of a faith.

That's why we feel the need to go back to the Bible, to discard present theology, and to figure out the changes that are urgently needed in our Christian language. How are we to interpret God's plan in the Bible and in history? How are we to bear witness to the unity of so divided a church? What do we have to offer to people whose courageous witness is a silent challenge to us? When have our theological reflections dealt with crucial problems of the present day? What do we have to say before events run their own course? I would like some bishops and theologians to spend at least a month in prison. There they might discover a reality that few of us experience and none of us discuss: *that grace is not the exclusive property of Christians but God's gift to any human being whatsoever.*

To get back to my initial subject, it's becoming evident to me that our Christian interpretations of the Bible and of history are not particularly true to the facts or to contemporary language. For example, the true story of Francis of Assisi has not yet been written. What we have so far is hagiography dripping with illuminism or plaintive piety or outright folklore. There is precious little truth in it. Francis of Assisi is turned into a medieval case history, and so he loses all his relevance and value for us, precisely because we cannot relate his life and deeds to the historical and structural conditions in which we are living today.

Clear proof of all this can be found in the unsuccessful attempt of Vatican II to express itself in an idiom intelligible to modern people. I reread the conciliar documents while I was preparing my court defense. It struck me that they sound fine to people who are used to scholastic terminology but have little to say to secularized non-Christians. Just try to explain them to a Marxist! They were supposed to have been incisive and crystal-clear, like a manifesto. Instead we end up with a conglomeration of paragraphs in which every statement is preceded by a repetition of the relevant articles of faith—as if they were afraid that something might be read or interpreted out of context. *Gaudium et Spes*, for example, which starts from an anthropological perspective, quickly gets lost in the repetition of dogmatic truths. It sticks to defining principles and never gets to practical guidelines. When will we find something to say about real life that will be more than the usual mumbo jumbo?

We must scrape the rust off theology, which has been dominated by stagnation since the Middle Ages. For three or four centuries we have been absorbing the thought of Thomas Aquinas without ever seeing what it signified for theological reflection in its own day. Confronted with the Renaissance and its innovative currents, we retreated—except for Luther, who had the courage to move forward. Confronted with the industrial revolution, we hurled anathemas. And in the face of scientific progress, we simply voice suspicion.

We haven't shown the daring of the church Fathers, of men like Augustine and Thomas Aquinas, who thought in theological terms about their own times. Only now are we beginning to wake up, very slowly, from a long dogmatic slumber. With Karl Rahner and moral theology, we may now have caught up with Kant. We still have to get past Hegel and when we do there will be many surprises. Now is the time for us to do what Thomas Aquinas did. He had the courage to take his lead from the philosophy of Aristotle. We must have the courage to give serious attention to the questions and contributions that Marxism has to offer to theology. We must try to harmonize the intellectual currents of our day just as Clement of Rome and Justin Martyr did in their day.

Well, Pedro, these are the ramblings of a prisoner who doesn't have many books around for backup support. We have just a few here. They bring us books from the monastery, but the censor often prohibits certain volumes. For example, we can't have books by Bultmann, Cullmann, or Cox. Perhaps it's precisely this lack of books, along with the many hours we have free for brain work, that leads us to reconsider the Christian life. I recall Bonhoeffer's experience and, on another level, Dostoyevsky's. Both spent time behind bars. Perhaps the interest of European Christians in Marxism grew out of the time they shared in the Resistance movement and in concentration camps.

When you have time, I would like you to write me something about the book of Job. Ernst Bloch wrote something about it, I think, when discussing atheism in the Bible. I'd be very curious to read that book, but I don't know if it's been translated into French. And Bonhoeffer mentions his love for the Psalms, particularly Psalms 3, 37, and 70, in *Letters and Papers from Prison*. If you can find the translations, please send them to me.

I wish you an Easter full of liberation. Never have I lived it so intensely, because this year I am living through the passion in my own flesh. Unfortunately, the military authorities won't let us experience it liturgically. We remain united with you and your community in this vigil of freedom, and I embrace you in hope and friendship.

27

To his brother Tony[30]

March 28

Dear Tony, your letter made me very happy. I particularly liked your drawing of the comet and the Easter egg. It's obvious that you are coming along in your studies.

I didn't have a chance to see the comet. That morning I got up at 5:00 A.M. to see it, but the sky was covered with clouds and I couldn't see any stars. Someday the comet will return, and we'll see it together. This time it passed by quickly because

God sent it to take a quick look at the world and see how we human beings are doing. It came early, while people were still sleeping, to make a quick inspection of the earth. But it didn't see any of the wars or starvation or fights—none of the bad things—because people were sleeping peacefully in their beds. It only saw the eyes of children who had stayed awake all night to see it. And the children's eyes were full of light and joy. So the comet toured the world, looking at children's eyes all over the world. It probably saw the almond eyes of little Japanese children too. Then it returned to God. But it didn't find God in heaven. It knew that God had come down to live in the hearts of children and poor people. So it sent news to God that everything was going fine on earth, that people were super, and that they weren't doing anything wrong. God was satisfied and told the comet that it could have a year's vacation before returning to earth. So the comet decided to take a vacation around Mars.

Happy Easter! The child Jesus lives in your heart. A big bear hug and a kiss to you from your brother.

28

To Pedro

March 28

Dear Friend, your letter was a great joy to all of us. It made us feel that we're not alone in this adventure and that our experience does have some positive value for the gospel.

That is enough to justify our imprisonment here. It's not important to know how long we're going to be here. The important thing is what will come of this seed sown in prison. Perhaps our real charism is to offer Christian witness behind bars, following in the footsteps of Saint Paul, who went from one prison to another. But only God knows that for sure. We are at peace because we know that we're following the path Jesus Christ marked out for his church. All the apostles experienced martyrdom. The primitive church wrote its history in prisons, with the blood that had been spilled in torture. Today we're offering a witness of hope, as well as faith, in the sense of being present to events in the world. From the moment that we discovered the eschatological dimension of revelation and theology, the historical perspective of our hope has been leading us here to prison.

When I first got to prison and was put in solitary confinement, I thought for a whole month that I would never get out alive. But I felt real joy at the thought that I was sacrificing myself for a hope. In other words I came to realize that the promise made to us in Abraham and Jesus is ineluctable. That promise is what gives our struggle its guarantee. I know that it isn't easy for the Christian community to accept what is happening now as the *normal thing*—without self-pity or perplexity, but rather with joy. But we only have to remember that in an earlier time Christians were called "atheists" and "disturbers of the peace." They were accused of idolatry, of holding orgies and sacrificing human flesh at their eucharistic gatherings. Today, unfortunately, many Christians think that Christianity is a "social order," rather than an attitude of questioning and protest within history. They tend to forget that Christians aren't obligated to particular ideologies, political parties, or historical projects, but rather to the task of fashioning the future where the kingdom lies. To this end, Christians can adopt particular convictions, but they must always be provisional and questioning, in this sense: that so long as there is one oppressed human being in the world, the Christian will confront, question, and combat this oppression.

At times this Christian attitude may coincide with a particular political conviction. That's to be expected as long as we live on earth and amid the events of history. You can't put your hand in water without getting it wet. There is no redemption without risk. For other Christians, though, faith is nothing but a code of middle-class morality that requires marital fidelity, going to Mass on Sunday, and praying to God when you're in trouble. These people believe in a God "above" and don't realize that God can be truly known only in Jesus Christ. Jesus Christ is the presence of God in history. This man had the

43

courage to break with the morality of the Pharisees in his preaching and his way of life. He challenged the established order and was condemned to death as an "agitator."

I met you last year in June at São Leopoldo, when you were teaching at Christus Sacerdos.[31] I was your student for a few hours when you gave that conference on contemporary religious life at the request of Father Mueller (a man transfigured by grace). I read your notes on the changes that took place in the transition from a cosmocentric religious mentality to a secularized anthropocentric mentality. Let's talk a little about this.

It's true that the phenomenon of secularization is evident on a worldwide scale. It's the product of the industrial revolution, which caused a cultural revolution. But I am also convinced that secularization, interpreted in these terms, applies only to a highly developed technological society, like Europe or North America. It is undeniable that people today no longer view the world in religious terms and that their thrust toward autonomy becomes more and more evident. But I am afraid that certain authors want to *transform Christianity into a product that will sell well.* There is no doubt that talking on the telephone and driving an automobile and shopping at the supermarket and playing bridge on Saturday night have something to do with faith in God—that in these acts we either draw closer to God or move further away from him. It is also true that being close to God does not require acts of heroism, prolonged fasting, all-night vigils, or imprisonment. We must certainly rid ourselves of the notion that holiness is something exceptional, something fashioned out of extraordinary deeds and moments. But we cannot forget that Christianity is the awareness of a promise and that this awareness presupposes certain basic attitudes toward history. So what is involved, it seems to me, is not just a new secularized mentality and a new language to deal with the problem of God. Also involved is the existentially eschatological meaning of Christianity.

What does Jesus mean when he says that we are not of the world? Or Paul, when he says we must not conform to the world? To me they are saying that Christianity means nonconformity with the *saeculum*, with the here and now of history. They aren't referring to the planet earth as such. So we are not a secularized presence in history; rather, we are the irruption of the divine into secular society. I prefer to speak of the secularization of Christians, not the secularization of the world, insofar as Christians proclaim and bear witness to the eschatological promise. For only we, thanks to divine revelation, have any certainty about what does not yet exist, about the presence of God who has broken into human history.

So it makes sense to talk about secularization in a church that had shut itself up in the sacred. But I'm afraid that secularization will become only a problem of language, of mentality and habits, with a view to adapting to the *saeculum*. The *saeculum* aspires to the sacred, and our presence in it signifies challenge and protest and questioning—never conformity. That is why Christianity is the religion of the poor, of the proletariat, of the exploited class that is always the negation of the established order. The middle class can see Christianity only as an individualistic morality, because their concern is to maintain the status quo, which they call "Christian," as if Christianity were a force for resisting the dynamism of history. By the very nature and structure of their outlook, on the other hand, the poor are better able to receive and live the gospel, because nothing ties them to the here and now. Precisely because of their inner freedom, the poor are filled with hope and expectation, with a will to change and an incomparable capacity for sacrifice, service, and love. But we must present them with a Christianity that is praxis and not just a body of doctrines and liturgical gestures. The person who undergoes conversion cannot continue to live as before.

I hope to talk more about this praxis in my next letter to you. Please take what I've said as opinion, not as certainty. The only certainty is the uncertainty of our questioning. Regards to your community. Pray for our companions here in prison, anonymous martyrs of hope. Celebrate Mass for us, since the military authorities will not let us. In joy.

45

29

March 29

My Dear Friends, I wish you all the happiness I feel on this day of the Resurrection. The season is sharing my joy because the day has been bright, blue, and full of life. At dawn we sang and prayed for everything in us and around us that is making the passover from sorrow to joy, from prison to freedom, from uninvolvement to struggle, from death to life. Together we read several passages of the New Testament, particularly the letters St. Paul wrote from prison. Then we divided a huge Easter egg among us. It was as big as a football and filled with chocolates. Coqueiro strummed the guitar, while the members of our makeshift choir sang and the rest kept time with spoons, pots, and pans. The only sadness was the absence of Giorgio,[32] who is probably living the Passion in his own body at DOPS.

I'm sure that this is the Holy Week I have lived most intensely. Placed in a situation similar to Christ's, we participate more vividly and truly in his sufferings. They are prolonged in us: "Hard-pressed on every side, we are never hemmed in; bewildered, we are never at our wits' end; hunted, we are never abandoned to our fate; struck down, we are not left to die. Wherever we go we carry death with us in our body, the death that Jesus died, that in this body also life may reveal itself, the life that Jesus lives" (2 Cor 4:8–10).

Easter, which is liberation, has not yet arrived for us, who are prisoners in Christ. It is important that it arrive first for the church, that our imprisonment help to liberate God's word from every kind of subjugation and compromise. That is our mission, and we shouldn't grieve over it. It must be carried out to the end.

But all this is also an occasion of joy for us. We rejoice that we are able to suffer for Christ, that we can trust in him who has promised us victory. His resurrection bears witness to that victory. What good would our faith be if Christ had not been raised from the dead? Today I see my life as something very small in space and time. It acquires significance solely in the context of death and resurrection (. . .).

30

To Pedro

March 29

Dear Pedro, a happy Easter to you and your community. May it truly be a passover toward freedom on the long road before us.

It's not a matter of winning, but simply of regaining the ground lost by a church tied into money, prestige, and power. Because of this alliance the church didn't have to work for a living and resided in palatial mansions. Now the church is turning toward the poor, toward their yearnings and their struggles. Now it is working for a living, and so it is calumniated, maltreated, and put into prison. That's the way it has always been in history, and that's how it will always be. We are a part of the church living in prison. We don't give in to discouragement or surrender. We're grateful and happy to be here in this situation. We face insecurity, calumny, and torture; but we also experience unity, solidarity, constant prayer, and deepening charity. Our life depends solely on hope and on the complete support of our families and the most aware members of the church. All this is precious, and we keep going back to reflect on its essential elements. We ponder the reality of life, eternal life, and of death, which is the precondition for life. It is the mystery of Christ's death and resurrection: What matters is life, but death is the pathway to it. Once again we're in the novitiate, to begin anew. Never have I felt more like a priest offering sacrifice or like a religious offering witness. I can only convey a hint of our hope. It's impossible to say it all. A big hug to you and the others.

31

Dear Pedro, we got the notes you sent us. They'll be a big help to us, and we'll use them as a foundation for our own thinking. We have the facts, or rather, we are the facts, and your notes will help us understand them in the light of faith. Our prison experience is too important to be restricted to a few people in a short time. It will take much sorrow and sacrifice before the church as a whole manages to purify itself sufficiently to assimilate this experience, which belongs not only to us who are physically imprisoned here, but really to the whole church. Right now the church is dumbfounded, but in time it will understand and respond to the sacrifice of Christ.

We have been happy here, as if in a new and unexpected novitiate. There are fifty of us in a cell hardly big enough for twenty. We have only one shower. The atrocious condition of this prison has been reported to the judge of the Civil Court. We have tried to improve things: We do our own cooking; we try to keep the cell sanitary; our families bring us food; we make up pastimes; we "improve our minds"; we pray and study theology. We don't let ourselves give in to desperation, and we find ourselves being restored continually (. . .).

32

To his parents

March 31

Dearest Mom and Dad, I would be very happy if you could look at everything that is happening to me from my own point of view, which is the point of view of faith, of abandonment to God's plans, of service to our people, to history. We were born and raised in a middle-class environment, where you always have to preserve appearances. By now I could have had my B.A. and been earning a good salary on some newspaper,

48

secure in the esteem and admiration that certain people had for me before they learned what choices I've made. But none of that has anything to do with my vocation as a Christian. History is not built on appearances but on choices. You have to choose, and you can't please two opposing sides. Either you align yourself with the poor and the oppressed, or you acquire the badge of the oppressor. You have to live either by human logic and common sense or by the impulses of the Spirit.

I know how hard it is to live for the future. Those who live in the past and wish at all cost to preserve the present (as if they could) do all they can to destroy us. They heap lies, abuse, and threats on us, and they take away our freedom. But they can't make us stumble into contradictions. We must be courageous and consistent. We must commit ourselves to the future because God's promises are there. The book of Genesis tells us that Abraham, out of faith in God's promise, forsook his native land and his wealth to journey to the promised land, a land flowing with milk and honey. That journey symbolizes the attitude of the Christian. Jesus came to proclaim the kingdom of justice and peace to us. Each of us in our own way, according to the abilities we have been given, contributes to the making of this kingdom and the quest for it. The kingdom can not be established outside history, so our journey toward it must take place within history (. . .).

33

To Marco, a student friend

April 7

Dear Marco, those who know that they have to stay here a long time are more relaxed. They follow a schedule, a program of study, and so they continue to live their lives. They don't waste time recalling the past or dreaming of some imminent, utopian future. They integrate their activities into the rhythm of life that you can establish in prison. As far as our personal life is concerned, the rhythm of prison life can be as intense and productive as our pattern of living outside. Idleness is the most dangerous temptation facing a prisoner. It is what turns prison into a school for crime for ordinary prisoners. Lacking any formal education and unable to devote himself to reading, the average inmate spends the whole day sleeping, rehashing the past, and talking nonsense. Abandoned to his own uselessness, he wears himself out day by day. (There is no chance for rehabilitation because our prison system is punitive rather than corrective.) His only prospect is to learn new techniques of theft and crime from his cellmates.

We can hear the conversations in the other cell block. They shout to each other from cell to cell, always in underworld slang and never using their real names. They use nicknames so that there is no danger of being informed on. (. . .) If one of them doesn't have a nickname, he is labelled by the place he comes from. They usually sleep all day and sing all evening, banging out the rhythm of their songs. (. . .) The most curious thing of theirs is the *teresa*. It's a looped string that they use to pass objects from one cell to another. If a person can handle the *teresa* well, he can do wondrous feats. For example, a prisoner may throw a cigarette down the corridor, so that it stops right in front of the intended recipient. But then a prisoner in another cell shoots out his *teresa* and lassoes it for himself. Another easily learned technique is sign language. If you want to talk to someone at night, you use sign language so you don't wake up other prisoners (. . .).

34

To a community of nuns

April 7

(. . .) Our lawyer came to see us. He had no news about our trial. He told us that the public prosecutor, Durval Airton de Moura, was studying it "attentively and sympathetically." In general, the handling of cases in the Second Tribunal is a slow process. There are people arrested a year ago who are only now being interrogated. If our cases are heard in the order in which we were arrested we will not come to trial before next year.

It's a curious thing that after you have spent a certain amount of time in prison, your lawyer has nothing new to say when he comes. He functions much like a doctor at the bedside of a chronically ill patient. All he can offer is consolation. He has no remedies to offer. He can try to give some idea of the complicated juridical and penal mechanisms and how they work, and he can try to lighten our pessimism a bit. Many people look for a confessor, not to be pardoned but to unburden themselves. Even though our lawyer can't function directly in the trial process, the very fact that we know he exists and that he comes here is a source of great comfort.

The other day I was talking to the mother of M.C., my companion in prison who is presently on trial in Rio, charged with participating in the kidnapping of the U.S. ambassador. (There, it seems, he confessed that he was the one who struck the ambassador on the head with a gun butt. He never told us that.) I have always been greatly impressed by this woman's composure in the face of her son's imprisonment. In Rio some officials tried to shake her by saying that M. would be sentenced to death or life imprisonment. She answered very calmly: "That does not bother me. It is as if my son had cancer. However much people try, they cannot find a cure today. But perhaps we will discover one very soon. In any case being in prison is better than having cancer."

To change the subject, we have sent the TV back. I'm glad because now we have at least a little quiet in the cell after supper (. . .).

All of us here thank you for the Easter greetings. You are always in our prayers. Pray for all prisoners, especially for those who are living the Passion of Jesus Christ in their own flesh. A big hug to you all.

35

To his brothers and sisters

April 7

(. . .) It's gotten cold, and now it's hard to get out of bed in the morning. I get up around 6:30 A.M. and devote an hour to yoga. It's the best thing I've discovered here in prison. N., who is a yoga teacher, is a fellow prisoner in our cell. Every day he directs my exercises. We're divided into two groups, one exercising at nine, the other at ten. I prefer to get up early and do the exercises by myself, because I have more time available to me then. Yoga movements are supposed to be very slow, and it's all based on breathing. Traditional gymnastics help build up the muscles, but yoga helps develop endurance, makes the body supple, increases our control over our bodies, and develops concentration, emotional balance, and sound health. Another advantage is that it isn't tiring, because all the movements are slow and follow the rhythm of normal breathing. Little by little I'm learning to correct a whole series of mistakes that we inflict on our bodies. You should never breathe with your mouth and lungs; you should breathe with your nose and diaphragm. I've stopped using a pillow, and I'm learning to rest for a few minutes with my head down because it's a mistake not to let blood flow to the brain. Over time these mistakes may help to cause arteriosclerosis. My nervous tension disappears if I manage to concentrate for a few minutes, interrupting my breathing and then resuming its normal rhythm. In this way I correct the cardiac alterations provoked by emotion or fear and completely regain a sense of tranquility. In short I'm finding yoga to be a wonderful source of all kinds of miracles. I need only mention that it allows its practitioners in the Himalayas to walk around naked in the snow and control their body temperature by their breathing (. . .).

Once again we hear that we'll be transferred to Taubate next month. Nothing is certain right now, but it could happen. That would be the fourth prison I would get to know (. . .).

36

To his brother Leo

April 7

Leo, buddy, today is your birthday, isn't it? I send you a big bear hug, but I'm sending it by mail. If I tried to deliver it in person, you would probably ambush me with a judo chop.

(. . .) Today is a great day for us Brazilians. Not only is it your birthday. It's also the day we commemorate Tiradentes.[33] (. . .) He fought against those who wished to tyrannize Brazil, and he died on the gallows for his love of justice and freedom. Funny, isn't it? In every age the people who fight for freedom end up in prison, and some of them are condemned to death by the judges of their day. I wonder what would happen to Tiradentes today? It seems ironic that Tiradentes, an early martyr for our freedom, should have this penitentiary named after him. Wherever he is now, I'm sure he's none too happy about that. But the prison, to commemorate its namesake worthily, could open its gates—or at least permit visits outside!

Tomorrow we commemorate a great date: the "finding" of Brazil by the Portuguese. Some philologists (Aurelio Buarque de Holanda, for example) distinguish between "finding" and "discovering." I'm not exactly sure what the distinction is, but I have the feeling that neither word fits the underlying concept. "Finding" implies that Brazil already existed as a country before the Portuguese ended up here one fine day. But in reality all that existed before the Portuguese came was an immense expanse of land inhabited by Indians, and only a mistake in navigation landed Cabral[34] on our shores (although today some people claim that he left Portugal with the explicit intention of "discovering" Brazil). History's funny, isn't it?

Tell everyone at home that my lawyer comes to see me regularly. He had forwarded an appeal to the Supreme Military Tribunal requesting our release on bail, but at the last minute he changed his mind and withdrew the request. As I

53

hear the story, he realized that there was no chance for success. The report about us was highly unfavorable and drew quite a disagreeable picture of us poor creatures. Anticipating defeat, he retreated. (. . .) Now we are waiting for the charge being drawn up by the public prosecutor on the basis of the police investigation. In all likelihood we'll be charged on the basis of Articles 18, 23, and 25 of the national security law. But it is worth noting that almost all political prisoners are accused of violating those same Articles.

The bishops are fully informed of our situation.

37

To his parents

April 8

(. . .) It was the first time I had been out on the street since I came here last December. The journey from the prison to DOPS is a quick one, and you don't get to see a whole lot. I tried to imagine that the streets had changed, but actually everything was as before: the people, the cars, the weather, the polluted air of São Paulo. The city goes on living its own life oblivious to us prisoners and to the dead. I suddenly realized that I never really have had any tie to this city, even though I worked in it for three years. It has always remained alien to me, as characterless as its cold, grey skies and totally devoid of any charm. I passed through it as if it were a terrible figment of the imagination that kept disappearing and reappearing from a world of shadows.

I realized clearly that my world is different now. Five months in prison and the prospect of remaining here for some years have put real distance between me and the outside world with its schedules and obligations, work days and vacations, sunny days and moonlit nights, noisy streets and flowering gardens. My present world is made up of bars, of high walls guarded by machine guns, of cells lit even by day with electric lights, of meetings with my lawyer, and of young faces marked by sorrow and yearning for freedom. It's a world all its own, in which the imagination has full scope and we feel the living inner pulse of history.

Does a prisoner get used to prison? No, no one gets used to being deprived of freedom, which is always stronger than our patience. I would say rather that a prisoner adapts to prison life, which does not totally lack a rhythm of its own and which does have a certain interest. Anybody who doesn't adapt lapses into laziness, desperation, and moral debility. My expectations include the fact of prison, and so far I have been able to face it with my head held high. The important thing is not to let it overwhelm me (. . .).

38

To Pedro

April 11

Dear Pedro, I too find it strange that the clergy are so worried about the problems of celibacy and professional life. Such concerns might well be primary in Europe, but it's clear that here we still haven't cut the umbilical cord and are living in the shadow of the Old World. We forget that our reality is totally different and imposes its own peculiar tasks and concerns on us. It is not right that in an underdeveloped country like ours, on a continent in political and social ferment, the clergy should meet to discuss personal problems. It seems to me that this is not the response people expect from us. Does it perhaps signify a lack of the gospel spirit and apostolic aspirations?

In one of my last letters to you, I focused on the problem of Christian "praxis." Let me try to sketch out a few ideas on the subject. Contemporary philosophy is trying to tell us that a human being is essentially defined as a practical being, that is, as someone who transforms reality by work and action. The history of humankind is a history of praxis. And when we talk about a human being, we talk about his works and deeds, which give him definition and fulfillment. History is entirely the result of human action. People do not exist on the margins of history and praxis, and history does not exist as some suprahuman, autonomous force. Humankind and history are inseparable. Indeed, we come to know God's revelation only through history, only through what he communicates to us of himself. A German philosopher stressed that history does nothing, that it is the actions of human beings pursuing their objectives. Human beings transform reality and themselves, and the story of these transformations is the real history. Every human being wittingly or unwittingly engages in praxis. Sometimes we act instinctively, seeking personal objectives without thinking ahead to the social impact of the action. So we have the common laborer, for example, who works to live and never thinks about the oppressive nature of the productive process with which he collaborates. Others engage in praxis that is consistent with some consciously held objective, and their intentions are in a certain sense directed toward the objectives of their actions. In any case the determining factor in practical activity is the result—what objectively happens as the fruit of this activity. A work of art cannot be judged by the intentions of its maker; it must be judged on its objective merit. For it is the practical result that counts: Sanctity does not consist of good intentions. Charity is fundamentally action.

I think that Christianity is praxis, first and foremost. It would be valueless if it were just a doctrine or a religious theory. A discourse on God (theology) would produce little that was meaningful.

According to the Old Testament, God's revelation is the revelation of a plan. Its elements unfold through the historical praxis of the people of God. In and through the objective results of this praxis, the people become aware of the divine word. The divine word is equivalent to action; the awareness is identified with love. The authors of the sacred book were sufficiently inspired to be able to read the plan of history. God is present, and God is guiding us: These are the two data derived from the actions of God's people. The inspired author does not theorize the praxis; he notes it, points it out, and demonstrates the divine activity present in it.

The Gospels too are the fashioning of a praxis. Jesus is seen to be much more concerned with teaching criteria of life than truths of faith. Almost all his parables are designed to stimulate a new way of behaving and living. He is implacable against the Pharisees, who do not act as they teach. He himself bears witness through his actions. He summons people to be aware, to be committed and courageous, to have faith, hope, and much love. This being the case, we cannot talk about instinctive praxis in the case of the Christian. The gospel embodies the example and the *conscious awareness* that should direct our actions. It is a criterion of life. Our fidelity to this criterion is confirmed by our capacity for self-giving, for loving, and for acting; and this action takes place in history, in the ongoing eschatological process.

It seems a very serious matter to me that we Christians today have lost this evangelical praxis. We are not even aware of its importance. We have religious habits, customs, and practices. Our spirits are lulled by the truths of faith in which we believe. But we have no practical activity in which we objectify our faith in all that has been communicated by God. Why? Perhaps the roots of this quietism are to be found somewhere in the Middle Ages. Medieval Christendom, characterized by *ratio, auctoritas, ordo universalis,* by speculative theology dealing in celestial categories, lost its apostolic vitality. It sought to preserve the Christian faith and the society that professed it, putting all its energy into the fight against heresy. Christians went on the defensive. But historical progress is stronger than forces for mere preservation. All unprepared, the church was faced with schism, the moral decadence of the clergy, and growing inner contradictions.

So this historical period left us with two things. On the one hand it left us with defensive apologetics (if you will pardon the redundancy); on the other hand it transmitted to us a body of crystal-clear doctrine. Since then we have been circling around that body of doctrine, so absorbed in it that we have only recently opened our eyes and caught sight of earthly realities.

Even today we Christians still lack an operative praxis that might transform and sanctify history. We lack it first of all because we are not consciously aware of the historical process. Despite the example of the Old Testament, this awareness is still reserved to a small elite in the church. And second, we lack such a praxis because we are used to using doctrine as our sole point of reference. Our doctrine provides us with all our answers—except that it does not tell us how to live with concrete facts. Third, we do not have such a praxis because we consider the society in which we live to be Christian.

Action requires a point of departure and a point of arrival. But where do we want to go? What are the chief objectives of the church today in a world devastated by famine and war? What is the aim of pastoral activity here in Brazil? It cannot remain on the level of mere intentions, as purely subjective activity. The point of departure (the original intention) and the goal (the practical result) are never equivalent. The created work of art seen by the public is never the artist's original vision. It is the working out and development of his intention in action that determines its objective effect. Isn't Christian life today a bit like subjective intention?

For example, you meet with a group of Christians in your parish. They read the Bible, study a little theology, learn to think about it. These Christians are consciously aware of and responsible toward their religious obligations. But don't you sense that something is missing? Specifically, some way of objectifying everything that they are pondering and assimilating, some praxis with spelled out methods and objectives that enables them to be as one with what they do?

We often say that the Christian is supposed to transform the world. But where do we prepare for this activity? In what Christian community can people learn to prepare the leaven that makes the bread rise? If we grant that Christian life does not admit a gap between intention and result, between subjective and objective, then we must grant that intentions are proved on the level of practical action. This action must not be spontaneous, naive, subjective, "spiritual." It must be consciously aware, critical, objective, and "material." In other words it must be capable of altering the present for the sake of an eschatological future that is already partly realized in the individual, physical future of each one of us.

As you can see, my dear friend, there is a whirlwind of ideas in my head. But they all are at the level of intuitions. I cannot systematize them in a critical way. I lack the theoretical framework since I was unable to acquire it during the years that I have dedicated to action. My activity was often very disorganized, but it was also rich in experiences and discoveries. Perhaps in the years of prison that lie ahead I will be able to study more. At least I hope so!

We remain united in prayer. Our joy is the awareness of the "new" that is coming into being in this prison. A hug of friendship and gratitude to all of you.

39

To a community of nuns

April 11

(. . .) We got the notes you sent us, and we're reading them. I think this attempt to make theology understandable to the laity is great. In the monastery I constantly fought against the currents of intellectual perfectionism (the European malady). It seemed to me that we should divulge our knowledge, especially since the laity are interested in theology but are fed such pap.

Some of our lay cellmates are reading the notes, and they like them a lot. I hear you're carrying on your fine work of liturgical renewal. I saw that clearly when I went to Mass at your place last July. It seems to me that you've managed to form a solid parish community for worship and study. I hope your apostolic vitality continues to grow stronger all the time.

40

April 26

Dearest Mom and Dad, *Estado de São Paulo* printed the news of the pope's visit to Sardinia on the front page of yesterday's edition. He walked through the streets of Santo Elia, the poorest section of Cagliari, and stopped to talk to the residents. He went into the house of a very poor family and spoke with Signora Graziella Murcia, who was sick in bed. Overwhelmed with emotion, the only words she managed to say were: "Your Holiness, find my husband a job." The newspaper does not say whether the pope answered her in the affirmative. It simply says that he exhorted the woman to have faith in God and then blessed her. Then he gave a commemorative medal of the visit to her husband and a box of candy to her little girl.

This simple meeting seems highly significant to me. The newspaper says: "The Pope left the comfort of the Vatican and went to one of the poorest regions of Italy. For the first time the splendor of his trip was marred by the protests of anarchists, who regard this visit as an affront to the wretched poverty of the Sardinians." Willing to share "the joys and the hopes, the griefs and the anxieties of the men of this age, especially those who are poor or in any way afflicted" (*Gaudium et Spes*, no. 1), Paul VI was embarrassed when confronted with the clear, direct, and concrete request of this woman: a job for her husband. Notice that she did not ask the pope for a cure, for alms, or for prayers for her family. She asked for the minimum that a person needs to fulfill himself and to acquire life's barest necessities. She asked for a job.

The pope made a request of his own in Sardinia. He asked the rich not to close their hearts to the needs of their neighbors and to try to lighten the suffering of the starving. He reiterated in a way the persistent appeal of John XXIII—that the developed nations give more aid to the poor ones, and give it disinterestedly. (The total aid of the United States to underdeveloped nations does not amount to 1 percent of the national budget.)

What is the difference between Signora Murcia's request and Pope Paul's? As I see it, the woman asking a job for her husband embodies the appeal of poor people and nations who are tired of receiving alms and blessings from the church, who want the church to contribute to their betterment without paternalism. What they are asking of the pope is not the same thing that the pope is asking of the rich. Signora Murcia did not ask for a favor or for pity. A job is the minimum that a human being needs for food, clothing, shelter, and human dignity. It is a human being's right and duty. But that brings us to a question: Is it the task of the church to give work to the unemployed? It seems to me that it is not the church's specific mission to maintain an international employment agency. Its task is to act so that there may be work for all, to fight for a social structure that can make use of all the available manpower. In short, its task is to fashion a world that is in line with the kingdom of God.

This is what the poor expect now from the church. They want its active participation in solving their serious problems. Not that they expect it to operate as a political party or a government agency or a class organization. They want it, in its own way, to serve humanity and establish God's justice among people: "My brothers, what use is it for a man to say he has faith when he does nothing to show it? Can that faith save him? Suppose a brother or a sister is in rags with not enough food for the day, and one of you says, 'Good luck to you, keep yourselves warm, and have plenty to eat,' but does nothing to supply their bodily needs, what is the good of that?" (James 2:14–16). What did Jesus do when he was surrounded by a hungry crowd on the lake shore?

The pope, on his part, asks the rich to have compassion on the poor. Now his appeal, it seems to me, shows a lack of perspective typical of many Christians. He does not encourage the poor to fight for their rights—which would be much more consistent with the view that man is the active subject of history. Nor does he even perceive the overall dimensions of the problem: that this situation does not depend on the good or bad will of the rich but is the fruit of a complex social structure, that it is based on a solidly established system with its own laws that determine the rules of the game between oppressors and oppressed.

Let us suppose that a rich Sardinian decides to alleviate the sufferings of the poor in one area. He decides to replace their wretched hovels with fine new houses. How will he pay for them? With the profits he has obtained from the work of laborers whom he has paid far less than their work is worth. In reality the wages are a way of fixing, unjustly, the price of labor-power. Labor-power produces goods that are sold in the marketplace at a price much higher than the sum paid to the workers for producing them. Now with this money the rich Sardinian will build new houses. But this will entail an enormous loss for him because the new houses will not generate new sources of profit. This unprofitable expenditure could lead him into bankruptcy, thereby causing his laborers to be laid off. So the solution of one problem will only have generated another problem. The rich man is rich only because he operates within the framework of the existing production system. And this framework is determined by the capitalist structure that now prevails.

The tragedy of the poor will be solved only by altering this structure and these relationships of production.

The church maintains a huge system of charitable works. All of them have been forced to play the capitalist game—not for profit but for sheer survival. Insofar as they reject the rules of this game, they will go bankrupt. And insofar as they (or the rich man in Sardinia) alleviate the sufferings of some poor people, they will be collaborating in the rise of poverty. It is a vicious circle that can only be broken at its roots, by altering the whole framework of society's present system of production. When will we realize this? When will we come to see that this analysis is not tendentious or seditious but rather a true picture of the real situation?

You are quite right. We pray for those who are taking risks in outer space, forgetting those who are here on earth. But God help the astronauts if NASA relied solely on prayer! Faith must be fleshed out in works, says Saint James. What works do we propose?

Let us remain united in unbounded love for this church that is searching for its proper path.

41

Dear Mom and Dad, I just finished reading your last letter. I think your idea of contacting the bishops is excellent. But on the other hand I must recognize the fact that the cardinals are not yet capable of taking a public stand in our favor. The support of the church is undoubtedly great; but confronted with the kind of thing that happened to Tito, it is imperative to *say* something. That's why I think it's important for you to go to Brasilia. All the bishops of Brazil will be there, and the laity can take part in their meetings. The efforts of our "church in prison" are bent in one direction: We want the bishops to take a stand against the tortures and injustices practiced by the military government and in defense of the human person, and we want them to make a public statement to that effect at the end of the conference. If you go there, you will be able to help us by talking to bishops, priests, religious, and other lay people. Think about it. I don't know what approach you have used in your contacts, but we must coordinate our positions. For our part, we have tried to get the following points across in all our conversations and contacts with them:

1. We consider ourselves engaged in the struggle for justice.

2. We have never belonged to any subversive group.

3. Everything we have done proceeds from the requirements of the gospel.

It seems that they are not going to transfer us to Taubate. Everything is still very much up in the air. I'm just fine. A big hug to all.

42

May 4

Dear Teresa, today is an exceptionally fine and sunny day. I felt the sun on my own skin for the first time since I've been here.

There is a young man in our cell who must take the sun every day, on the doctor's orders. He cannot get down the stairs because his legs were injured at the time of his arrest. I carried him down into the courtyard and we stayed there together, enjoying the most beautiful sunshine in the world. I sweated as if I were in a Turkish bath. Too bad it doesn't happen more often. Funny—exactly six months ago at São Leopoldo it was a beautiful day just like today. I had gone swimming in the lake at the seminary, and right after my shower, as I was getting dressed, I was informed that the police were looking for me. I immediately undertook my famous flight, which made the front pages of the newspapers but didn't last very long.

But who can foresee the ways of the Lord?

I don't know to what extent your impatience is justified (. . .). Don't worry, I have no objections to your religious choice, whatever it may be. The important thing is to search always for the truth as honestly as you can, without illusions. I find you sincere in the matter of religion. If Catholicism is not convincing enough for you, then faith in God, love, and generous dedication to others can be found in other religions. The essential point is not to lock yourself into an egotistical, individualistic lifestyle. We are happy only when we manage to come out of ourselves and dedicate ourselves to others, even if the price of that happiness should be our precious liberty, which is life. For authentic life, Teresa, is the life that awaits us on the other side of death. All our hope should be placed there.

I pray for you. Much thanks for your letter and your friendship. A kiss of joy and peace.

43

To Silvia, his sister's friend

May 10

(. . .) Your letter is wonderful. You were really inspired when you wrote it. It's true that friendship unites people into a single family. It is born of common interests, personal affinities, and encounters. It is sacrifices that have put us into communion with each other. Behind bars friendship is an extraordinary force, even toward people on the outside. Today I know that I have made some solid friendships, that I am surrounded by people whom I love and who love me. The only thing that bothers me is that I can't talk with these people, but I also know that my imprisonment speaks to them more clearly than any words I could say.

The flowers! Thanks from all of us for the seven marvelous roses. They opened up into countless petals, then died yesterday. But they lived long enough to bring us a ray of light. It doesn't matter that they didn't last long. The important thing is that they had the courage not to stay closed up in their buds, that they were wise enough to come out of themselves and rise toward the sun in delicate red petals. They left the mark of your presence here.

44

To a community of nuns

May 10

Dear Friends, (. . .) I view the renewal of the church with a lot of optimism. But it will take great sacrifices, and afterward it will no longer be such an easy thing to be a Christian, for it will entail risk. It will require concrete actions and taking stands. It will no longer be the vague, quietist, religious sentimentality of people who remain fiercely attached to this world while they wait for the next (. . .).

45

To his brothers and sisters

May 10

Greetings to you all! The most beautiful gift I've gotten recently was Mom's visit, bringing Dad's written statement about my imprisonment. It is remarkable in both form and content. I have no changes to make, no criticism to offer. Among other things, it's well written. Mom and Dad have managed to express beautifully everything that has been happening to me in this dynamic period of church renewal. There is a direct relationship between that renewal and my imprisonment.

For centuries the church has justified the social order in which it has lived. The values of that social order (the family, private property, tradition, individual liberty, democratic government, etc.), were considered Christian. Social order and Christianity became so closely identified that we came to speak of "Western Christian civilization." In reality this was an ideological interpretation of Christianity propounded by those in power. And the social order, which created its own peculiar abuses, found the justification for its existence in this interpretation.

So Eisenhower (who was Protestant) sends troops into Vietnam "to defend the Catholic minority."

Cambodia is invaded and its population decimated "in defense of the free world."

In South Africa Christians appeal to the Bible to prove the divine origin of apartheid.

And here at home Archbishop Sigaud[35] can say, without risking the accusation of heresy, that the class divisions into rich and poor derive from the will of God, who did not desire equality among people.

Now, in this postconciliar period, our problem is to return to the sources and to see clearly that Christianity is not identical with any social order; that it challenges and questions all social orders; that the state does not represent any divine right, that

66

laws are made by people and these people are wholly concerned with protecting their own privileges.

So we will inevitably see a clash between Christianity and the social order, between the church and the state, between Christians animated by love and those who are attached to their laws (. . .).

46

To his parents

May 11

Dearest Mom and Dad, thanks for the letters. If I don't write more often, it's because there is not too much to talk about in prison. It's like living on a desert island, except that an island is surrounded by water and we're surrounded by bars. And it's deserted here. When I arrived at Tiradentes prison in December, there were about a hundred prisoners here. Now there are almost three hundred, and more on the way. There is an attempted bank robbery in São Paulo almost every day, and after the young robbers are arrested they end up here. Whether ordinary criminals or political offenders, they all come under the state security laws.

We prisoners come from every social class and walk of life. The most important prisoner is certainly Caio Prado Junior, sixty years of age, a publisher, printer, bookseller (the "Brasiliense" book stores), and author of several books. He was sentenced to four and a half years because of an interview he gave in '67. Here he's just a prisoner like the rest. He gets up early to get the bread and milk provided by the prison. He cooks his own meals and does his own laundry. There are no rich or poor in here. Everyone is treated alike, and everyone has the same rights. Whatever one prisoner gets from the outside is divided among all. The only real differences are of intellectual ability, but we try to minimize them. We give Portuguese and English lessons to anyone who is interested.

Any prisoner might become a really good card player. I've learned to play bridge. (. . .) It's the most common mental hygiene in prison, particularly in DOPS, where you're rarely allowed reading material and, even if you were, the nervous tension caused by the interrogations kills the desire to read.

Contrary to what you people outside might expect, time passes incredibly fast for us. I'm astounded whenever I count up the time. I've already been in prison for half a year! We owe this to the rhythm we've managed to impose on our lives here. I try not to sleep more than eight hours a day. (By the way, I'm the one who gets to sleep first in our cell; the period of absolute silence begins at 1:00 A.M. and ends at 9:00 A.M.) I go to bed around 10:00 P.M. and get up between 6:00 and 6:30 A.M. I pray, read the Psalms, do yoga, and drink coffee. Then I devote the whole morning to studying French, taking time out to read the *Estado de São Paulo*. Our big meal is at 12:30 P.M., and silence is compulsory until 3:00 P.M. I spend the afternoon studying theology. We don't get a snack in the afternoon. At 5:00 P.M. the others do gymnastics together, but I don't participate. After supper, around 7:30 P.M., I play cards or read a novel. At this time, almost all the radios are tuned to the classical music program on Eldorado station. Every now and then we dance the samba a bit to the accompaniment of two guitars. Yesterday, as a matter of fact, thanks to the rich repertoire of two of our companions, we recreated the history of popular music in Brazil from the beginning right up to the start of the *bossa nova*.

I think our life here is more or less like life on a submarine—except there are no white rabbits and no date set for surfacing. (I've stopped writing to say goodbye to Caio Prado, who has been transferred to barracks. I take back what I said about all prisoners being treated alike. But I don't see the advantage of being in prison by yourself, no matter where it is!)

I'm glad to hear from Mom that you're settled into your new house, but I'm sorry to hear that the name of the neighborhood was changed. The old name was much more tropical-sounding and filled with folklore.[36] (. . .)

If your baby boy isn't afraid of cockroaches, you can be sure that he will become a great animal breeder like his father, who spent his childhood taking care of his little zoo, while I devoted myself to rock music and became an habitué of the Minas Tennis Club.[37] But my playboy career was interrupted suddenly when I began to frequent the "six o'clock tea" at São Jose (. . .).[38]

A kiss for you all. I am writing you from cell seven on the eve of C.'s birthday, which is two days before we celebrate the liberation of the slaves. Waiting for my own liberation, I greet you all.

47

To Sister Monica, a Brazilian nun

May 12

Dearest Sister Monica, your candy has sweetened the bitter taste of prison. All this solidarity on the part of our fellow Christians reminds us of Saint Cyprian's account of his fellow Christians' efforts to alleviate the sufferings and bolster the hopes of those who were to undergo martyrdom and set an example for others.

Today we had a fraternal visit from the president of CELAM, Archbishop Avelar Brandão of Teresina. He came to demonstrate what we had already seen by the visits of the apostolic nuncio, Cardinal Scherer, and others: namely, the church stands by those who suffer—be it in poverty, abandonment, or prison. Human justice is not identical with the justice of God. We who are "a scandal to the Jews and an example of folly to the Gentiles" know that God has chosen the foolish to confound the wise of this world. So Paul tells us, and he spent a great deal of his time in prison.

We fear nothing; we regret nothing. Prison is our Mount Carmel. Our prayer becomes all the more real and alive as we come to realize that the Christian's proper place is with the poor and the oppressed, with those who experience injustice or suffer for their love of justice. That is the message of Vatican II and of the gospel. The person who is imprisoned, be it behind bars or in sin, needs our love, not our judgment. Faith is not given to us so that we may condemn, but rather so that we may save. Transgression of law can only be understood in the light of charity. As Jesus said, the Sabbath was made for man, not man for the Sabbath. That is what he tried to get across to the Pharisees, who in their religious myopia could only see the legalistic side of things.

We don't know how long we'll have to stay in prison. So far there is no formal charge against us. But this period has been rich in evangelical revitalization. No one can take away our peaceful conscience or our inner joy. Indeed, how can our present tribulations compare with the promise that was given us, the future that awaits us? "How deep I find thy thoughts, O God, how inexhaustible their themes!" (Ps. 139:17).

Accepting this mystery, we contemplate God's wonders. Following the Lord, even into prison, we find true freedom.

Keep us in your prayers. The "church in prison" is united with its brothers and sisters outside.

48

To Pedro

May 16

Dear Pedro, the only news from prison comes from our own experiences and thoughts. Today I've been thinking a great deal about these six months that I've been in prison to date. You on the outside, who have never experienced it (I would not wish it on you for the world!), cannot imagine what it is really like, however much I might write to you about it. Although I have been here for six months, I think it's too soon to make a definitive judgment. That will have to wait until I have been free again for two or three years. Only then will I be able to say something about the meaning of prison life and its impact on us.

Based on my brief experience so far, I must say that prison is an absurd institution. It is as ridiculous as burying a man alive. It does not punish, and it does not correct. Its sole objective is to remove from society those who have threatened the security of its "masters." Countless human beings have spent long years in prison and, on leaving, returned to the same life they had led before. Their imprisonment did not increase or diminish the security of those outside one bit. Nor did it serve as an example. The example was provided by the ideals for which these prisoners fought and for which others would take the same risks.

It is abominable that society feels obliged to confine the best of its youth, those capable of transcending self-interest and egotism, behind bars. A waiting room is a good image of what prison is like. You wait there, among total strangers, for your turn to come. You wait for hours, and after reading all the magazines and chewing over all your thoughts you suddenly realize that the waiting time is indeterminate and that it is impossible to leave the room. So your only recourse is to start up a conversation with the other people there. At the same time every detail in the waiting room takes on importance. After several days, you know the pattern in the tablecloth and the upholstery, and you could describe every detail of the room with your eyes closed. The people and things in the room become as intimately familiar as the parts of your own body. To make the interminable wait less awful, you make up a game: Everyone changes seats—and you rearrange the furniture—but you have no chance at all to make any decision that will change the basic situation. The door can only be opened from the outside; no one inside has a key.

In the past six months I have passed through three different prisons and experienced eight different cells. I came to know each one of them as well as I now know cell seven. Although there are fifty of us in here, I have no trouble at all in finding

71

something I need. I know exactly where everything can be found, just as I know for a fact that my fellow prisoners are capable of loving. Prison can humanize a person or turn him into a brute. It teaches us to love, to smile at suffering, to get over moments of depression, to nurture patiently the strength of our will and our ideals. On the other hand, prison can drive a person crazy (it has happened to two people here), crush his moral strength, or fill him with hatred and destructive impulses.

Living together is a great help. It lightens the burden for all. There are also moments of tension, when the atmosphere becomes charged and everyone is suddenly transformed with fearful expectation.

As for myself, I feel that something has grown inside me, something firmly rooted. It is as if I have emerged from fog and can now see things clearly. I can see what I want and why I want it. I can see my capabilities and what I am up to facing. I feel I have reached some point of no return, from which it would be suicide or treason to go back. I must go on without a backward glance. I no longer have anything to lose because everything I now possess is within me. All that is left to me is the road ahead. Even if it does not take me very far, every step will make a difference (. . .).

49

To his parents

May 20

Dearest Mom and Dad, last week the newspapers indicated that the charge against us would be published any day now—if we can rely on the statements of the public prosecutor. So far there is nothing, but I expect to see a new campaign of vilification against us in the press. They will say absurd things about us. It is war, after all.

I am anxious to know the outcome of the bishops' conference in Brasilia. They were supposed to issue a document on church-state relations. But I am not very optimistic even though eleven bishops of Goias[39] have published a denunciation of the harrassment of political prisoners (see Sunday's *Estado de São Paulo*). I think there will be behind-the-scenes negotiations between the bishops and the government at Brasilia. Our church is not yet sufficiently free. The final report issued by the conference will reveal whether or not our bishops stooped to compromise with the regime.

Something odd has been going on here in prison. It is public knowledge, and I believe I can tell you about it openly. Some half dozen political prisoners have given their support to the present government platform, which they believe to be nationalist and opposed to all imperialism—North American, Soviet, Cuban. One of this group went to Brasilia and spoke with Colonel Manso Neto. Now they go from cell to cell, expounding their point of view. They assert that the government will move toward democracy, the first step being the release of those political prisoners who were not involved in armed resistance. This first step is related to the government's concern to erase the terrible image it has acquired for itself abroad. My impression is that these young people are in fact smoothing the way for their own release. They say that one of them had already been condemned to twenty-eight years. But to me it doesn't seem a very honorable way to win back your freedom (. . .). The Christian should say straight yes or no, no halfway measures. We must be utterly consistent. But mercenaries crop up everywhere.

I have no other news. It's very hot, and the routine is the same as always.

Have you read the gospel? We can only give Caesar what concerns him: money. God gets everything else, including our lives. A kiss and a hug to be shared by all.

50

To his brothers and sisters

May 21

(. . .) The text of the charge against me has finally been made public in *Diario Popular*. It's long, but it doesn't say very much. There is no serious charge against me. But I realize that my activities in the south will be regarded as crimes so long as people are not convinced that helping the persecuted is a right and duty of the church. The last part of the charge says this: ". . . falls under the sanctions of Articles 14, 23, and 25 of Decretal Law 898 of September 29, 1969, Article 53 of the Military Penal Code, and Article 154 of the Federal Constitution of October 17, 1970 [which abolished political rights for ten years]." Dad can explain to you what all those numbers signify. All the Dominicans were indicted on the basis of those same articles. Now we are waiting for the preliminary hearings. They've charged 138 people in this case, but only fifty-six have been arrested.

(. . .) I don't think dad should accept job offers from the government unless they are purely administrative. I don't believe he has a vocation to be a politician. Past experience suggests where his true vocation lies (. . .). A big hug to you, and the assurance that you are in my prayers.

51

To his parents

May 31

(. . .) Mom's hopes for the bishops' meeting were not realized. The Spirit is stirring, but it is not strong. I was realistic about it from the start. I know our bishops well, and I know how far they are capable of going. They put together a declaration that was the product of countless emendations, and it ended up as a patchwork of cliches. In short it epitomizes what they themselves are: naive, lacking a vision of history, lacking theological training, and insensitive to the great problems of the country. They wrote to save themselves. They shouted, "Long live the king!" and handed us over to the secular arm (. . .). Ah, how history keeps repeating the same droll story! Not once does the word "poor" or any synonym for it crop up in their report. It doesn't much matter what they might or might not have said with regard to us. Our fate is sealed, and Caesar has marked us out for the arena. But it was important that they speak of those who have neither bread nor circuses, who are screaming with hunger in the Northeast, who build everything yet possess nothing. About these people, there is not a word, not a single word: ". . . indeed the state of the nation is well and continually improving, thanks to the government." Let us wash our hands of the matter. And they are received smilingly by the king, who hands out chocolates.

The newspapers inflated the Eucharistic Congress into a great event. The church and the government were buddy-buddy. But in the eyes of a Christian it was an exhibition of paganism "because he who says he loves God and does not love his fellow man is a liar." Many will be saved thanks to the sacrament of ignorance. X. described the document as "muddle-headed and obscene." During World War II housewives in the small towns of Germany complained of the soot pouring from the chimneys of the Nazi "factories." No one saw anything; the only evidence was the soot. When the Nazis were defeated, the world learned that these "factories" were camps where the Jews were exterminated. The "deputy"[40] had remained silent. The air we breathe today is polluted, but who takes note of it?

But Vatican II tells us that the church is not the bishops; it is the people of God united in Jesus Christ. When has the church ever made a mistake by allying itself with the future? My confidence in the Spirit is enormous. It is not for nothing that he has allowed us to end up in prison, not for any merit of our own but for our openness to the gospel.

I hope all goes well at home.

P.S. I recommend that you read Mounier's *Personalisme* and that you study his writings and personal experiences in the French Resistance.

52

To Pedro

June 1

Thanks to all of you for your letter and for the texts that you sent. I am very interested in learning how to read the Bible. I very much like the comments on Saint Paul. You stress a point that exegetes have not paid enough attention to so far: the social conduct of Jesus and his apostles. The attention of exegetes is always concentrated on the texts themselves or on discovering how the primitive community understood the message, without regard to the context. In other words they don't consider the social behavior of Jesus and his apostles as a source of revelation (even though nothing was explicitly said when Jesus stood before Herod). To be sure, Jesus spoke in terms peculiar to his age and nation, and it is therefore useless to look for an explicit program of social reform in the gospel. But with the help of modern scientific disciplines we can ascertain what Jesus' vision of the world was, in what way his preaching did denounce a slave society, and in what forms Greek philosophy influenced the primitive Christian message so that it acquired an ideological overlay (natural right, etc.) that it had not originally possessed. You only have to look at the doctrine of divine right of kings to see that Christianity assimilated extraneous ideological elements.

I am convinced that we are living through a propitious time for profound Christian renewal. It is one of those periods that in an earlier day gave rise to new religious orders. Today it is no longer a question of establishing new institutions. It is rather the moment to bear witness to a new spirit whose substance is summed up in the terms *metanoia* and *kenosis*. To me, the document approved by the bishops at the meeting in Brasilia summarizes the whole agony of the old church. Everything in that document lacks consistency and foundation. Nowhere in it do we find reference to "the poor" or any synonymous term. From beginning to end, the text deals with issues that are of no interest to the people: seminaries, vocations, the ecclesial tasks of the laity. At the end this mosaic of shock absorbers tries to gloss over the pressures to which the church is being subjected and to confirm the policy of "peaceful coexistence" with the regime. It is all very sad. Not to mention that bandaid, the Eucharistic Conference, which is the supreme expression of a country where faith has been reduced to performance of the sacraments.

We are fine here (. . .). We still have not received permission to celebrate or receive the sacraments. We have written to the bishop about this, but we have not yet received an answer.

Thanks to you all for the friendship you've shown us. Let us remain united in grace.

53

To his brothers and sisters

June 7

(. . .) The television set came back to our cell for the World Cup games. This evening Channel 13 announced that in Argentina the "dictator" Onganía[41] had been deposed. It's funny: Until yesterday he was called "president." Now that he has been deposed, he is called a dictator and will go down in history as such. Clearly no dictator ever considered himself as such, not even Hitler or Mussolini. While in power they are presidents or generals or prime ministers. We don't call things by their right names until they've been rendered harmless. Only when the mighty have fallen do they get the name they really deserve.

The same news report stated that the military junta that deposed the "dictator" would designate a new "president" for the country within ten days. One comes down, another goes up; the labels change but the poison in the bottle remains the same, as if calling the new dictator "president" would lighten the despotism and make him more popular. The people of Argentina will continue to be oppressed. They will not have the right to vote nor will they have any say in the destiny of their nation.

With Onganía out of power, I am sure the church will pay homage to the new ruler. It may even go so far as to say that he arrived in the nick of time "to free the country from tyranny." What phonies and liars people in power are!

Well, that's a problem for the people of Argentina. We're here in Brazil, well guarded in this penitentiary where even the dust beneath our feet is familiar to us by now (. . .).

Right now it's fashionable to play the artisan here. We are trying to help those families that are in dire straits because the breadwinner is imprisoned here with us. Some of us are making fine purses out of colored plastic cord, and others are making rugs. It's good work, and our group is becoming more and more creative. I'm going to try to cut down on studying a bit and get involved in the handicrafts. You never learn enough, and here in prison I've learned a great deal. Besides my personal development that only time will reveal, I've learned to cook pretty well and to use my bed as a mini-apartment. I now know how to wash a floor, do a little darning, study and pray in the midst of noise, read lying down without falling asleep, be courageous, and love people.

Cardinal Scherer and Bishop Fontana from the south stopped by here on their way back from Brasilia. They brought us news of the episcopal meeting. It's my impression that things may have gone a little better behind the scenes than appears in the official statement.

The bishops sent a letter expressing their solidarity with us in our sufferings. Yesterday Cardinal Rossi, however, gave an interview to *Estado de São Paulo* in which he said that our attitude, objectively speaking, had nothing to do with Christianity. As if Christianity consisted in going to Confession and Holy Communion, which Jesus never did. In fact he said: "Not everyone who cries 'Lord!' will enter the kingdom of heaven" (. . .).

I hope everything is well with you people. Here we're simply prisoners—no formal charges, no news.

My feeling is that "they" are more interested in giving us a taste of prison than in condemning us (I prefer not to say "judging" us). A hug to all.

54

Thanks for the letter and the things you sent me. We all were vaccinated against smallpox; as usual my vaccination didn't take. (. . .)

Tito went to court yesterday in connection with the UNE case.[42] He learned that all the Dominicans will be charged under Articles 22, 23, and 25 of the National Security Law. We expected as much, since almost all the prisoners here are charged under the same articles. We're waiting for a visit from our lawyer for further explanations, but he's sick right now. Article 25 seems to entail a minimum sentence of five years and a maximim sentence of fifteen years.

I don't want to frighten you with this next piece of news—in fact, I'm the one who should be frightened, but I can't help viewing it as a joke in really bad taste. This week a young man was sentenced to three years in prison for having taken part in a meeting at a friend's house where Marxism was discussed. Three years in prison for a meeting! He'd been in prison for nine months, and he felt so sure of acquittal that on the day of sentencing he packed his bag to go home. This incident will give you some idea of the uncertainty that afflicts both lawyers and clients in our cases. The law says that a charge must be published within two weeks of the conclusion of the formal inquiry. Four months have already passed!

In the future when people talk about these things, they'll ask one question: Where was the church? Why did the church say nothing? It's not that I want the church to defend me but it ought to defend human rights, to aid the advancement of the poor, to combat injustice [censored].

The same question must be asked with regard to Germany, where six million Jews were murdered without anyone "noticing." It's what *The Deputy* is all about. It must also be asked about Vietnam because so far the church has not been able to say which side is right in that war.

This is the politics of silence, the sin of omission. Many will have to pay for the words that were not spoken and the deeds that were not done. It's all right to debate theoretical principles, but to be frightened by the hard facts is inexcusable.

It's rainy and quite cold. Lucky for those who don't have to leave their houses on a day like today! (. . .).

55

To Pedro

June 28

Dear Pedro, I don't think prison conditions will allow me to pursue my studies in theology as I had hoped. You need a guide, a library, and a little peace and quiet. Here our reading is often interrupted, and we have very little space in which you can be alone and create a little "distance" for yourself. So we must adapt to circumstances, make the best use we can of the few books we have, and discuss the more important theological themes among ourselves. Individual reflection and group discussion here bring out aspects of Christian experience that are usually not explored adequately. The fact is that we're living through a period of thoroughgoing renewal on every level of human activity. We might use the expression "new church" to convey the reality of this attempt to recapture the pristine aspects of Christian living, the aspects that came into the world with the preaching and witness of Christ and his apostles. I prefer not to use any adjective at all when I refer to the church. It has remained one and the same through two thousand years, undergoing constant renewal as it strives for greater self-identity. I believe that the renewal we are experiencing today will be the most profound and complete since the Council of Trent. For in a certain sense it is a "radical" renewal, full of innovations that are revelations to some people and heresies to others.

The renewal officially recognized by the church in the sixteenth century had its beginnings in the twelfth and thirteenth centuries. It took three hundred years for official doctrine to absorb the ideas and experiences that on first encounter aroused indignation and scandal. For example consider the impact of the theological reform of Saint Thomas Aquinas, which was based on the pagan philosophy of Aristotle. Church renewal always follows the same sequence: The Holy Spirit sets various charisms in motion, overthrowing concepts and institutions held definitive until then. Afterward these charisms are understood and assimilated into Christian faith and the teaching of the church. It is useless to try to find a direct and immediate connection between revelation and comprehension. Even the apostles, who were inspired, were unable to comprehend some aspects of the revelation transmitted to them by Jesus Christ.

Today we decry the Inquisition, which once was hailed as a way of bringing the faithful to salvation. Almost no one was able to understand the mystical life of Saint John of the Cross. His own confreres kept him in prison on a diet of bread and water. It's the same old story: What the past judged as evil is in the future acclaimed as good and vice versa. The history of the church is filled with examples of this. Wasn't Joan of Arc condemned to the stake by a commission of theologians?

In any period of church renewal one of the greatest difficulties is to distinguish faith from culture. Some elements of faith are absolute, definitive, and indisputable, such as the dignity of the human person. Other beliefs, which pass for elements of faith, are only constructs specific to a particular culture and period, like the identification of democracy with Christianity. It's obvious that this distinction occurs on various levels, and that faith always acquires a specific cultural expression as the faith-of-human-beings-living-in-history. The praxis of the faith is always clothed in a particular idiom that is the expression of a given culture. The danger lies in our ready tendency to generalize our own cultural values as if they were elements of Christian revelation. Progress, material well-being, prestige, and power are major values in our culture. From childhood we are taught that "to succeed in life" means to acquire a respectable social position, preferably one with a good income attached. Our culture is so imbued with this standard that we treat wage-earners and common laborers as "different" from ourselves. When advertisers wish to sell a product, they suggest that owning it is synonymous with power and prestige. Even the church is influenced by this scale of values, which has nothing to do with Christianity. The parish priest in some small town in the interior tries to stress the power and grandeur of the church by building a cathedral. Bishops live in mansions, and curates want their own Volkswagens, though such lifestyles conflict with the evangelical dictate of poverty, which should be the church's witness even more than its inner spirit. I don't mean to suggest that progress and material well-being are antievangelical in themselves. But when they belong to a small minority at the expense of the majority of the people, they are antievangelical.

What exactly is a true element of faith? Renouncing one's self-interest for the sake of one's neighbor is. Consider God's own example in Jesus Christ. He was born in a stable; he was a common laborer; he formed a community of uneducated men; he had no place to lay his head; he died on a cross between two thieves. Today, in a world where the vast majority of people are poor, I am convinced that the church should live entirely like them and identify itself wholly with their interests and aspirations. Our stately edifices and luxurious mansions are senseless, as are our classical culture and our bourgeois trappings. None of these things is an authentic sign. None of them will bring human beings to conversion to Jesus Christ. None of them breaks down the barriers of social class that we help to build up and are afraid to destroy, as if social differences between human beings are evangelical while social equality is not.

Facing this reality in this spirit, I don't find prison a burden. Prison is full of the poor, and now events have led us to identify with them. This is the home of those who have nothing, not even their freedom. Christ himself passed through this place and with him many others who would not accept injustice. It doesn't matter that now we are not understood, that we have to stay here for who knows how long. The important thing is that none of this will go for naught; in time it will contribute to the renewal of the church and the world (. . .).

56

Dear Pedro, all my thanks for your letters. I seem to gain courage from confidence and solidarity. Such gestures are very important to us now, for we are surprised by the silence and fear pervading the world outside this prison. Everyone seems to be waiting for it to "pass," as though it were a bad dream, not reality. Meanwhile people tend their cattle, count their money, and keep out of trouble.

We live in a world ruled by prudence, abstract principles, and idealistic notions. It's as if reality didn't exist or were neatly circumscribed by the satisfied consciences of the lazy. It's ridiculous to argue about the color of the walls after the house has caught fire.

Today, up to my neck in the tragic reality of prison, which is the quintessence of a whole current historical process, I realize to what extent the church is off target for lack of information and a proper perception of the facts. What does the church really know about transportation policy, foreign investments in our country, the distribution of electric power? Practically nothing, because churchmen are formed in a culture that is artificial for our age. They cannot deal with a technological project or an economic reality without first setting up a strict scale of values that distorts the facts. For many years we saw people only as contrite penitents kneeling in our confessionals to recite their litany of sins. We exalt the individual at the expense of the group. We can't believe the data of the social sciences because we don't take part in the production process. We don't work for wages. We're accustomed to reasoning from theories rather than facts.

Long live formal logic! The indispensable transformation of the church is too thorough to be accomplished quickly. But when it is done, the change will be radical. It will not just modify our ecclesiastical structures; it will mostly alter our mental categories, which have been infected by a whole cultural atmosphere that proclaims certain values as if they were a re-creation of Christian doctrine. That's why we stand about debating ends and means while history moves on without asking our permission or even our opinion. As if means could be predetermined without reference to praxis! As if a priori principles could be applied without reference to the objective conditions that determine the ways in which principles can be put into practice.

It's painful to see the church keep repeating the same principles without ever applying them. It talks about justice, freedom, and people's participation in the decision-making process, about the countless rights that are noted, recalled, and exalted in all the writings and teachings of the church. Meanwhile the government of Ecuador turns sharply to the right and no one says anything, although this would be the occasion for the church to practice what it preaches. The United States invades Cambodia and bombs the civilian population and no one says anything, although this would be the occasion for the church to practice what it preaches. Last year two hundred billion dollars were spent on armaments and no one says anything, although this would be the occasion for the church to practice what it preaches.

In short we keep silent in the face of facts. Or else we give the government a vote of confidence, forgetting that no nation or government is going to renounce its privileges in favor of a justice that it doesn't even perceive. Holy Innocence!

I am sure that *metanoia* will touch many people and that the ways of the world will change. We must give it time to happen. . . .

57

To his brothers and sisters

July 7

(. . .) The newspapers have published the charge against the Dominicans. It begins with a summary statement of various papal teachings, well chosen to prove how heretical we are.

It's interesting to note that according to the indictment we are more heretical than subversive. The public prosecutor spelled out the chief aim of the Dominican order (to fight the Albigensian heresy) and then pointed out how far we have strayed from that purely religious work. The one thing he forgot to mention, or perhaps didn't even realize, is that the Albigensians denied the human nature of Christ whereas the Dominicans taught that Christ was a human being in history. This precludes a Christianity devoid of incarnation and alien to the problems of this earth.

The text of the indictment notes that the accused Dominicans were living in an apartment in the underworld section of São Paulo. It fails to point out that near their apartment stood the Church of the Consolation and the Ministry of Justice. The indictment also notes with a trace of sadness that we didn't save the lost sheep that abound in that neighborhood. But this observation seems even more applicable to the local parish priest, who is specifically responsible for the souls in those particular bodies.

The charge will be formally registered next week. V. and C. were let out on bail. That's good because they had begun to feel the burden of prison life and were often depressed. Usually this happens to people who do not manage to figure out the real reason for their imprisonment. I'm the only one left of those who were arrested in the south. It's only fair, in my opinion, because I feel sole responsibility for everything that happened there.

The publication of the charge suggests that the preliminary hearing will take place soon, but it doesn't tell us anything about the sentencing. There are people here who were charged and found guilty a year ago and still haven't been sentenced. So I think this affair will drag on for a long time (. . .). An affectionate hug to all.

58

To a group of young Christians[43]

July 18

Dear Friends, (. . .) I owe you a letter but my hands have been busy with long hours of manual labor. To help out the families of poor political prisoners we've been making leather and plastic purses, ornamented rosaries, and embroidered wool rugs. Our cell has been turned into a crafts shop where everyone gets in on the work. The rate of production is reasonable, or at least good enough to keep some families from being evicted. We have the advantage of being able to work when we please, so we can work long hours. There are people who think that in prison irresponsibility is the rule because, closed in as we are, we cannot feel responsibility, but only anxieties that render us impotent. But that's not true. Wherever you find yourself, even on a desert island, you can create your own rhythm of work and impose on yourself set tasks.

I've been in prison since last November, and I can truly say that I haven't noticed the time pass. I'm so organized that I go to bed every evening contemplating the things I'm going to do the next day: finish reading a book, write a letter, or make a plastic purse. The great danger in prison is idleness, laziness, and lack of interest in the little things that make up your life here. The prisoner who starts counting off the days is lost (. . .). In that sense I may be lucky not to have been sentenced yet. I have an unspecified amount of time to spend in prison, and that doesn't upset me. At least I feel certain that I won't die in prison!

In your letter you speak of the work of Martin Luther King, Jr. I admire him too because he was able to make choices and give of himself, to die for love of others. But I confess that I'm not convinced of the validity, or rather, of the efficacy of his methods. Look at Gandhi: admirable, meritorious, but useless from the viewpoint of history. India has changed little. The power once exercised by the British is now wielded by the Americans.

A better world won't be fashioned by isolated initiatives, good intentions, and charismatic individuals. A better society is a joint endeavor for all those who want it and wait for it. It's hard to learn to swim without getting into the water.

I think, for example, of the social encyclicals. They're full of suggestions for improving human life in accordance with Christian inspiration. But they're ineffectual suggestions because you can't take medicine without its affecting your whole body. And it sometimes happens that certain chronic infections can be cured only by surgery—even against the will of the frightened patient.

The newspapers have already published the charge against us. Oddly enough, the text tends to emphasize the "theological" motifs of the charge by citing old church documents and isolated papal statements. I seem to be in Joan of Arc's situation, although I don't recognize the theologian who opposes me. It's interesting to see how history twists and turns and always returns to the same old ironies. Yet people never learn.

There are 138 of us listed in the indictment, of whom only fifty-six are in prison. The rest are on the run. Can you imagine how long it will take to question, charge, and try all these people? And on the day of the Last Judgment we will go over it all again. But Saint Paul says that patience breeds hope, and hope is even greater than patience. This gives us courage (. . .).

We are very grateful for your kindness. I think this is only the beginning of a friendship that will continue to grow. I join you in prayer and praise to the Lord.

59

To his brothers and sisters

July 28

I got the letter you sent this week. It's become less cold here the past few days, but I still haven't worked up the courage to do my gymnastic exercises. I'd rather wait till summer. In the meantime I'm doing a lot of studying and reading, even some novels by Machado de Assis[44] that I chanced to find.

Our lawyer hasn't put in an appearance lately. Now he's on vacation with his family. There's no additional word on the trial either. The court is overloaded with work.

The routine of prison life goes on: handicrafts, reading, conversation, cooking. Every once in a while we play cards out of sheer boredom. Cards were useful at DOPS, where there was nothing to do while waiting for the interrogators but fiddle with an old, frayed deck of cards. Now we have improvised a ping-pong table of sorts—improvisation being characteristic of prison life—and it works fine. We play with great gusto.

It's strange to see how human beings adapt to their circumstances. I remember the miners of Morro Velho[45] who were so used to the mine that the sun bothered them when they came out into the daylight. Suffice it to say that every Wednesday, when visiting hours are over, most of us go right to bed when we get back to the cell. We feel as tired as if we had just taken a long hike. I think a lot of things will bother us when we get out of here. I've heard of one such case of a person who got out of prison, went to eat in a restaurant, and couldn't stand "that racket." The fact is that here you get used to a strange silence, broken only by the same familiar noises, and you forget the typical hubbub of life on the outside. All your senses adapt, some improving and some deteriorating. Your sense of hearing grows very sharp—you can make out faint noises far away. Your vision deteriorates a bit, due to the lack of sunlight and the constant use of electric light for reading.

As far as my birthday goes, I can't think of a thing I need. I want for nothing. I have too many clothes as it is. It's pretty hard to choose a gift for a prison inmate! I think the best thing, if anyone is coming, would be to bring food. Anything will do. If you want to come on Saturday, call the lawyer's office so he can get the permit. A big hug.

60

August 7

Dearest Mom and Dad, it's too bad you didn't come. We had prepared a reception worthy of you (. . .) but the permit didn't arrive. In any case, Teresa's visit helped to allay the homesickness. It's good to see people from the "outside world" in here. In that sense my cell is a privileged place, because if we climb up on the bunk next to the barred window we can see the comings and goings on the street and not forget what cars look like. Really, this isn't my style, because I am not the nostalgic type who moons about the past. I prefer to tackle the present, even if it's terrible, and look toward the future. So this cell—160 square meters with bunks everywhere—and the forty-one people living in it now constitute my intense little world.

I know that many people outside think that we inmates idle away most of our time, feeling no sense of responsibility and doing nothing useful. It's not true. Something like that may occur during the first few days in prison, caused by the initial shock and the constraint of a new and strange way of life.

Here in prison, waiting (for what?), you learn many things. In particular you learn to respect other people. You begin to feel that the fellowship that can exist between human beings can work miracles. That's the source of your hope and your patience. Right now I'm in the "clergy corner"—three beds where we meet in the evenings to pray, read the Bible, talk, and tell jokes. Since we don't have any beer, we're eating the candy that Teresa brought and a few biscuits snitched from the pantry, along with a cup of tea. We talk about A.'s shirt, which is so old and threadbare that it looks like a spider's web. But he's terribly attached to it! He has other shirts, but he prefers that one. But the joke can't go on much longer because the shirt is on the verge of disintegration and A.'s sentence will be up on September 28. My release date will be around the turn of the century, when prisons will have become museum pieces. I wonder what people living in the future will think when they hear that human beings once imprisoned their fellows? (. . .)

61

Dearest Mom and Dad, I must confess that I too was impressed by the impact of the soccer world championship. Our cell is on the fourth floor, and through the bars I watched people running happily through the streets. It seemed as if a new ingredient had rendered joy more explosive: The winning of the Cup, which has by now acquired a mythic value of its own, has become the object of the contest. This Cup has become a goddess, desired and worshiped by players and fans alike. From all over the country, fans come as if on pagan pilgrimage to the Cup.

In this outpouring I see the emptiness in which our nation and its people live. We have to go back to the decadence of pagan Rome to find similar excitement over a circus spectacle. Any nation whose glory is the physical prowess and athletic ability of twenty-two human beings is in a bad way. It would be all right if the game constituted relaxation after productive labor, but that is not the case. Soccer lures crowds to the stadium, stimulates discussion everywhere, and turns the players into idols and national heroes. It's a clear indication of the mood and temperature of the country.

This phenomenon of pagan religious idolatry is more common among us than we might like to think. We gravitate toward abstract values, even in the realm of interpersonal relationships. It is a phenomenon called "reification." Things, mere objects, acquire in our minds a value unrelated to their utility. Ownership of an automobile signifies social superiority, for example. By the same token human relationships are reduced to the level of things: An individual's importance is proportional to his money and material goods. We confuse the human person with his function; the function stands for and is the person. This is the cause of so much inner repression and neurosis and imbalance. This is the reason for all the safety valves we create to ease the profound loneliness and tension in which we live. I think we have reached the saturation point. Half-way cures and preventive measures no longer work for a malady that has become chronic. Clearly the culture we have absorbed has provided us with values only fit for blackmailers. We used to believe that the principles of the gospel could continue to exist perfectly well in this disordered mosaic. We thought we could straighten out the mosaic simply by shifting the pieces around a bit. Now we know that such an approach won't work; it would be like trying to use fireflies for lamps. The fact is that the mosaic doesn't work anymore. Time has shattered it, and its underlying framework has fallen apart. We must create a new mosaic with new pieces because the gospel tells us that we cannot put new wine into old wine-skins. (. . .)

62

To his brother Luiz Fernando

August 11

(. . .) Last Saturday we had an unexpected visit from the apostolic nuncio. He was accompanied by Monsignor Expedito, secretary to Cardinal Rossi. They brought us Brazilian cigarettes and a package of medallions with pictures of Pope Paul VI and Our Lady of Perpetual Help. They said they had ordered American cigarettes, but they hadn't come in time.

We distributed the gifts among our fellow prisoners and then had a good two-hour conversation. The nuncio said he'd asked the minister of justice to expedite our case, and it seems that they just might do that. The nuncio also requested that we be set free on bail, but that was turned down. The minister of justice promised that our case would go as smoothly as possible. The nuncio also said that you people had come to see him and that he had appreciated your visit. We talked about the problems of the church in Brazil, exchanging ideas on clerical renewal and the apostolic task of Christians. He told some interesting stories about his experiences as apostolic nuncio in other countries. Now he is about to leave for Canada, where he will perform the marriage of a boy whom he baptized. Then he will go to Rome, hoping to discuss our case with the pope. He promised to come to see us again when he returned to Brazil. (. . .)

Cardinal Pellegrino passed through Brazil and wanted to see us, but he didn't receive authorization in time. (. . .)

Our lawyer has not shown up since his vacation ended. When he comes, I'll ask him about the visiting permit for the twenty-fifth. Let me know who's planning to come, because each visitor must be named in the permit. (. . .)

63

To his brother Tony

August 20

Tony, your letter made me very happy. You write very well, and your penmanship is excellent.

Do you know the story of the king who called a meeting to find out who could describe the wonders of the universe using the least number of letters? Many wise men entered the contest. One wrote a book on all of nature: sea, rocks, air, fire, land, plants, animals, and people. Another described the seven wonders of the world, like the Great Wall of China, the pyramids, and the Temple of Diana. And so it went, each wise man trying to describe the things that impressed him most in the world. The king ended up with a mountain of paper containing descriptions of countless things. As he was plowing his way through all this, he suddenly noticed one small sheet of paper on which was written: A B C D E F G H I J K L M N O P Q R S T U V W X Y Z. He realized that all the wonders of the world could be described with these twenty-six letters. He summoned the wise man who had submitted that sheet and gave him the prize: his daughter's hand in marriage. The wise man married the princess and lived happily ever after. A bear-hug for you.

64

To Cristiana

August 27

I've never met you, Cristiana, and yet we're already friends. Thanks for your letter. Teresa told me about you in her last letter. You say that the important thing is to *feel* what is happening. Well, I have really *felt* everything that's happened to me. Despite the bars prison is a good thermometer for taking the human temperature. In the near future human beings will find it absurd that people used to confine other people in cages, and set armed guards to watch these cages of unarmed prisoners, simply because they differed in ideology.

From all this I conclude that freedom is not always physical. Outside prison are many "free" people who are really prisoners of themselves. And many people remain wondrously free even in prison. It all depends on your attitude toward life. One of these days I shall find myself in the defendant's box in court, accused of conspiring against society and wanting to change the existing order. There in court I shall recall many things: Brazil's magnificent landscape—and its slums; girls parading in beauty contests like cattle at auction; movies that teach us that the world turns on sex and violence; garden-city villas and low-cost IAPI houses; Chacrinha's[46] TV program that mocks humanity; newspapers with obituary notices set in large type to be read by a peaceable population. I shall call to mind that kings are no longer recognized by popular acclaim but by their coats of arms. I shall call to mind that this is the society we live in, and perhaps it is I who have made a mistake by taking all this too seriously. And I shall come back to prison, condemned, because this society fears me.

The important thing, Cristiana, is that there's meaning in

93

everything that's happened to me. Life doesn't end at the prison gate. It surmounts prison walls and pulses inside me. You can't imprison the spirit any more than you can imprison a human being in whose spirit is faith and a relationship with Jesus Christ.

Thanks for your greetings and your friendship. I embrace you.

65

To a religious community

August 29

(. . .) I was delighted to get your letter and I thank you for your good wishes. Soon it will be the first anniversary of the day of my arrest. (And still neither trial nor sentence by the Military Tribunal.)

I no longer expect these things to happen quickly. I'm prepared to wait a long time without losing my joy or good humor. I feel that my spirit is tougher than the bars that surround it. I am not living for the day of my release, for that would be a great waste of energy. My life now has a rhythm made up almost exclusively of intellectual activity. I'm trying to put this time of seclusion to good use. I do not trust the justice of men as much as I trust that time will make everything clear. It would be presumptuous to ask that the ways of God be comprehensible to everyone at the same time! For many people God's ways remain a question mark. In my mind and heart I feel certain that I've chosen the right road. I was always aware that it would be hard and dangerous.

Thanks for your concern and your solidarity with us.

66

To his parents

August 30

Dearest Mom and Dad, I was delighted with the letter you sent. It shows that you understand and are on my side in everything that concerns me. I admire and appreciate your intention to raise the little ones in the spirit of justice and social equality. They should know everything that's being said about me, including what's written in the press. They should have an overall view of reality and be able to judge it for themselves. I believe that people of firm convictions will always be able to face life's conflicts and struggles. Such people will be able to live by their own choices, not merely to survive by the whims of fortune.

During the long interrogations to which I was subjected, I tried to sort out my convictions, which are based on my faith, against the background of a world in which all is not well. I wasn't concerned about how others would judge them. I had kept in mind only the words of Christ, himself a prisoner condemned: "Blessed are you when people persecute you and say all manner of falsehood about you for my sake. The time is coming when those who kill you will feel that they are blessed by God." It would be naive of me to think that I could make a Christian choice without travelling the road to the cross. Today I'm convinced that this road, instead of destroying you, renders you more worthy and noble. What really destroys a person, even in the midst of seeming security, is lack of a clear path.

My imprisonment has some odd aspects. From the very beginning I tried to keep calm and in shape. I'm just not cut out to play the tragic role of prisoner at the bar of justice. When I was transferred from Porto Alegre to São Paulo, I came on an FAB plane, handcuffed and guarded by six soldiers with machine guns. These precautions seemed a bit exaggerated. The thing that worried me was that we might hit an air pocket, the plane would start to shake, the soldiers would lose control over their triggers, and I would end up looking like a sieve. Deciding that the shortest point between two human beings was speech, I started to talk to the guards. I asked them how the guns worked. To explain, they had to point the gun barrels away from me. Then I asked them about their work, and pretty soon they were sharing their afternoon snack with me. When the officer in charge noticed the change in atmosphere between us, he told them they could put down their guns and take off their helmets. The handcuffs were left on, so I had to make sure I moved both arms in the same direction. Otherwise I felt a terrible pull on my wrists.

I still haven't managed to figure out the reason for all those security measures at three thousand meters above the ground. But such happenings have taught me that there is always a considerable distance between a human being and the work he does—a distance we often fail to notice or to admit. At bottom in all of us, soldiers or not, are certain existential concerns and a way of being that are unrelated to the activities we perform. We are always looking for understanding, human communication, and love (except for the hopeless cases among us). So I have always tried to discover the human being in the soldier or policeman interrogating me, even while clearly recognizing the ideological differences between us.

In Porto Alegre I was interrogated by a colonel in the First Army Corps. In no time at all he was telling me about his family and children, and we were exchanging ideas on child-rearing. At that point, I tried to convince him that the level of TV programming left much to be desired in a supposedly highly cultured society. Programs that exploit the public's sado-masochistic tendencies do so, not for their own sakes, but to attract the largest possible audience for their commercials. How can a society be well balanced if the communications media dispense nothing but violence and sex? We are still far from the desired ideal.

The truth is that people still imprison other people. Future generations will find this as incredible as we find slavery or racial discrimination today. It will be up to your children to fashion an ideal world. It will have been worth it to face all this if they and their generation come to realize that everything must evolve, that nothing can be forever. We are being sacrificed by those who persist in trying to stop the passage of time.

Thanks for your good wishes. A trusting hug to you all.

67

To a religious community

August 31

Dear Friends, thanks for the birthday wishes you sent me. As Heidegger would put it, I have progressed a bit further in life and also a bit further toward death. Each day that we live, we die a little. Faith enables us to penetrate this mystery and see its true dimensions. Vilaça,[47] one of those bohemian Christians found only in Europe, writes that there are three things that we lack courage to look in the face: sun, death, and self. As for me, though I haven't the deliberate courage of a fireman, I've managed to face myself and death. I have not yet looked at the sun (which isn't looking at me right now, either).

I saw myself for the first time during the novitiate, back in 1966. It was a tough nut to crack, but also one of the most intense and fruitful periods of my life. It was not easy to give up my busy, itinerant life in Catholic Action and resign myself to the anonymity of the novitiate. It seemed as if the circus grounds had emptied and suddenly there were no longer any spectators to watch the show. I had to let go of the illusions and face the realities of my choice of the religious life. I had to look at my future stripped of make-up and costumes. I saw then that it was not exactly what I had imagined, that the religious life was not a great adventure or an esthetic pleasure but first and foremost a life of witness, a thoroughgoing commitment to the faith. That was precisely what I lacked: real faith, a personal encounter with Christ, a certain inner conviction that this was my road. Doubts. Suffocating obscurity.

For many months I saw nothing, believed nothing. I seemed to be at a crossroads without signposts or directions. I had lived so many years as a layman, had discovered and talked and written about the role of the laity. Vatican II had exalted the role of the laity in the world and the church. And amid all this emphasis on the temporal, on the world, on the laity and its mission in the church, I had chosen the religious life. Why? Wasn't I taking a step backwards?

The obscurity of my situation kept me from thinking. I was simply there in my white habit, listening to the lectures of the novice master and tending the monastery garden. But it was all strange to me, like a bad dream in which events seem disjointed. I was looking for Christ and faith, and Christ withdrew from me, hiding himself, absurdly, in the eucharistic mystery. The liturgy seemed to me to be well made esthetically, but devoid of content. There was a steel wall between us that prevented communication.

Out of pride, a pride that I still have, I refused to look back, to accept defeat. This same pride also kept me from progressing, however falteringly. My confessor at the time was Father Martino. I confessed my doubts and my resistance to him. His answer was simple—banal, even—but it had its effect: "When you are lost in a forest at night, you shouldn't go forward or back. It's better to stop where you are and wait for daylight."

And so I did. I stopped and waited, not knowing exactly for what. The first ray of light came to me from an anthology of comments by the church Fathers on the Holy Spirit. Then I immersed myself in the mystics, John of the Cross and Teresa of Avila. Saint Teresa has had considerable influence on my life as a Christian. She was proud like me, and she is the person I most admire in the life of the church. No one has spoken to me so powerfully and pointedly as she has. When I was arrested at Porto Alegre, the first book I asked for was one of hers.

In the final phase of my novitiate my vision became not only clear but transparent. I savored the faith—all of it, the sweet and the bitter. Even today I am still looking for the intimacy that God granted me then, in the calm following the storm.

In the novitiate I looked myself straight in the eye for the first time. It was associated with my choice of the religious life. I was not interested in its superficial features, which are often mistaken for its essence. I was looking for a total encounter with Christ, looking to place myself totally at the service of the gospel. The Dominican order was simply the means by which I intended to reach my goal. I have always tried not to confuse one thing with another, not to identify ends with means.

Vatican II and my experience in Catholic Action had helped me a great deal. I wasn't used to blind obedience without dialogue or respecting rubrics as sacraments. I had never been overawed by classical culture. I was not devoted to reading the commentators on Thomas Aquinas or the old treatises. My preference has always been for people like Congar, Rahner, Chenu, Ratzinger, Schillebeeckx, Teilhard de Chardin, and De Lubac. But even so I have never felt a calling to be an intellectual, to do research and scholarly study. I have always read under the pressure of some immediate need, and this has left gaps in my intellectual training. My studies and my whole life have been oriented toward action. I am a person in search of effectiveness, a sort of theological technocrat. I am always interested in knowing how to apply something, how to communicate something, how to achieve concrete results, how to determine praxis. And at the same time I lug about with me an intense longing for the contemplative life.

This first period of encounter with myself lasted until I got to prison. Here a second period of encounter has begun, with new data, stages, and prospects. Real-life experience has always had great value in my eyes. Everything I have learned so far has come to me from experience, and only through experience can I assimilate it. It has become a game for me, sometimes a dangerous game, from which I derive my joys and in which I face great obstacles. Of these I am not afraid, because they are part of the game. They're not purely accidental interruptions disturbing the ordered sequence of proper moves; they are part of the game itself. Since I know the key to the game, I play optimistically, believing in victory and converting obstacles into strategic retreats that pave the way for further moves forward.

Today it seems I have a peculiar need to talk about myself (. . .).

68

To a religious community

September 7

(. . .) I have my doubts about this highly touted process of renewal. What exists, in fact, is an awareness of the need for renewal, a realization that we cannot go on as before and must seek out new forms, perspectives, and stimuli. But there is a gap between awareness and action, and so far we have not bridged it. As is normal in this first stage, our actions are still imprecise, tentative, and experimental. In reality there is no renewal yet; there are inquiries, attempts, initiatives. You cannot make qualitative alterations (leaving behind age-old forms) without feeling remorse or nostalgia, without feeling somewhat envious of our predecessors, whose world was untroubled by our problems and questions.

Insofar as the religious life is concerned, I think we must ask a basic question that deserves a precise answer: Why renew it at all? Something that is doing well does not need to be modified or altered. I think there is only one answer to the question: We must renew it because we have lost apostolic effectiveness. Our life and witness and preaching, our way of expressing faith and showing love, no longer say anything to the people of our time. Or perhaps it would be more correct to say that they speak only to a certain social class, to which our preaching is not a threat, an alarm, or a call to conversion. Our witness, in the final analysis, is of interest to this class because it serves to defend and safeguard its present status.

We have come to realize that we must step outside our cloisters, that we must let down the drawbridge between our monasteries and the world, that we must identify ourselves with the people of our time, particularly the poor. We have become aware that we have lost our apostolic effectiveness and have become religious professionals. We have acquired a certain social status, a source of income, and a means of survival, all of which have nothing to do with Christ's summons. We realize that there is an abyss between our vocation and intention on the one hand and our actions on the other. Our preaching is without effect, our witness meaningless to the present generation, and our methods inadequate for preaching the word of God. We realize that our methods must be totally revamped if God's word is to touch people. We must redefine our objectives in today's world.

So we have set off toward renewal, only to find ourselves riding madly in all directions at once. Some of us have taken off our traditional habits or abandoned our cloisters. Others have patched up the defects in their training with the aid of psychoanalysis, university education, or some of the countless courses in renewal now available in such profusion. Others have become secularized professionals, rejecting every form of clericalism. Some have abandoned the religious life, become laicized, married. There has been some kind of change in all areas: liturgy, pastoral work, theology, and so on. Today every parish priest has his own liturgy, his own kind of preaching, his own catechetical orientation; every confessor uses his own approach with his penitents. The same questions receive many different answers, some more careful than others.

All this is quite natural at the start of a period of renewal, particularly when it goes hand in hand with a clerical emancipation proclamation. And yet I cannot help asking myself: Are we really on the right road? Will we really achieve apostolic effectiveness? Will our witness engage future generations and restore the confidence of the poor in us?

My impression is that it will not if renewal is restricted to form. If renewal simply means community life outside the cloister, the abandonment of clerical garb, jobs within the system that obviate our dependence on alms, then we will have altered appearances but renewed nothing. A parish priest may take to appearing in shirtsleeves, telling jokes and unburdening his soul to his parishioners, and still, all this notwithstanding, cling to the same vision of the world and the same purposes that he held before.

What counts, in other words, is not appearance but content. What really must be profoundly changed is not our dress or our lodging but our outlook and attitude, as people of faith, toward the world and history. It is not that our lifestyle has caused us to lose apostolic effectiveness but rather that our actions and our lives no longer convey the power of Christ's gospel message. All the renewal, theological and otherwise, will profit us nothing if it does not move us to act. Here lies the key to all the renewal that must take place. Moving into action implies *metanoia:* that is, breaking with the past, undergoing conversion, and adhering to a new vision. Awareness and courage are indispensable. Many have the awareness. They talk incessantly about justice, poverty, human liberation. What they lack is courage to create the conditions that would make renewal possible. They do not have the courage to recognize and admit that a true church of the gospel cannot exist within present-day social structures, that such a church must come into conflict with these structures. They do not have the courage to acknowledge the harsh reality that we live in a materialistic society whose conditions do not permit people to find fulfillment in God.

This last point is particularly noteworthy. The materialism surrounding us does not originate in ideology but in practice. In our consumer society, people are reified. Things have as much value as people, if not more. The essential goals of the culture that is our matrix are embodied in profit, power, and prestige. There is an explicit denial of God, although religion is accepted to the extent that it forms part of a system for neutralizing frustrations generated by the fact that, for most of us, work is self-sacrifice rather than self-fulfillment. This materialism, which shrewdly manipulates religion, is far more harmful than the ideological materialism that denies God, because it tends to create a situation in which Christians actively or passively acquiesce in glaring social evil.

The conversion or renewal of religious life will be logical and evangelical to the extent that it transforms the causes of our passivity. Apostolic effectiveness will be achieved only when our view of life and our attitude toward this world have changed. It will be achieved only when our identification with the poor is transformed from utopian ideal into social reality. For only then will we be able to respond adequately to Christ's summons.

Pray for us. Pray for all who are prisoners, inside and outside prison walls.

69

To the Dominican community in São Paulo

September 7

(. . .) Thanks for your good wishes and for the New Testament published by the monks of Taizé. It's the best translation I've ever seen. Who is distributing it? We would like a few more copies, because there are other people here besides our group who would like to read it.

I finished *O nariz do morto* by Vilaça. It's hard to classify it in a few words. The book represents an important step taken by the author: He has broken with religious atavisms and has opened himself wholly to the world. When I met him in Rio, he seemed a timid, introspective type who could not say a word about himself. Now he stands revealed; he can even talk about his failings, his uncertainty, and his doubts. But there are too many quotations in the book, as if he wanted to show off his erudition. His analyses are restricted to situations in which he has been personally involved; they deal with effects but don't ever delve into causes. Perhaps that's typical of autobiographical writing. But the book is well written, in a pleasing and poetic style. The part that struck me most forcibly was his autopsy of the religious life, particularly his account of past experiences with the Benedictines. Life with the Dominicans is less cruel. But it makes you ask: What's the sense of such a harsh and methodical rhythm of life, apparently lacking any perspective, if it is not to be found in prayer and contemplation? I find the contemplative life to be valid today, but it must be based on new models. It seems to me that the passivity of which he speaks in his book is quite pervasive in the religious life today, even more so than it was in the past. Chance stimuli come along to rouse people from it (. . .).

103

70

To Pedro

(. . .) You're right in your observation that my comments on church history place little emphasis on the mystery of the Resurrection. My true concern has been with the mystery of the Cross, which is for me the axis of Christian life on earth, according to the eschatological promise. The hellenic conception of God (Parmenides' "eternal present" of being, Plato's "supreme idea," Aristotle's "unmoved mover") is probably too far removed from the God of "the promise." Contemporary historical awareness has lost sight of the historical Christ, when in fact it is only his historical dimension that enables me to know something about God. In other words what I must know about God is precisely that which he makes manifest in Jesus Christ. And Jesus doesn't define the attributes of God. God is our Father, with whom we have a relationship of obedience and love. Everything I can learn about the import of this obedience and love is shown to me by Jesus Christ. The God I know about is the God living on earth, and this clearly contradicts all these divine attributes that sent medieval people into ecstasies. Jesus is a poor, limited, powerless, suffering human being, who submitted to death on a cross. The legitimacy and grandeur of this *kenosis* is proved to me by Christ's resurrection, by his victory over death. But only through this *kenosis* can I find and come to know God.

On page 5 of my essay you'll find an explanation of what I'm trying to say. The Protestant reformers said that the kingdom of God is to be found *sub cruce et sub contrario*. By this they meant that the kingdom of God is here, hidden under its opposite: Its freedom lies concealed under loss of freedom, its happiness under suffering, its righteousness under injustice, its omnipotence under frailty, and its glory under marred appearances. In the cross God is denied, yet he affirms himself in and through this very denial. So the banquet is prepared for the blind, the halt, the poor, and the sick—for the dregs of humankind. We will find God insofar as we are capable of choosing the humiliating pathway of Christ, impelled by the Resurrection, which is the apogee of this mystery, the affirmation in the denial, the hope into which our faith is translated. The Resurrection is the indispensable experience on this pathway that entails death but leads to life. In this sense, the only self-affirmation lies in self-abnegating; the only exaltation lies in humility; the only riches lie in discarding all one has; and only those who suffer can experience divine happiness.

I intended to make all this clear in my essay even though I did not explicitly point to the Resurrection as apogee. The contradiction of the Cross seems to me to be fundamental in the Christian mystery. It encompasses the whole praxis of Christianity: its renunciation, its questioning, its identification with everything that says no to the superficial values of modern culture. It is the contradiction between *pneuma* ("spirit") and *sarx* ("flesh") in Saint Paul's writings. It is the restoration of Christ as the one and only access to the mystery of God. The real obstacle to our rediscovery of the Cross is our lack of faith in the Resurrection. Christianity has been turned into the ideological basis of modern culture. Insofar as Christianity has been identified with the values of this culture, it has lost its openness to the future, its note of eschatological expectation, its dynamic hope in the divine promise that is being fulfilled in history. The world has imprisoned us in a closed circle: Our achievements have been deified, and we have lost the meaning of the Exodus and fallen prey to the worst possible kind of utopianism—the utopianism of the status quo. And all this has been blessed by the silent, static God of Greek metaphysics whom we have transformed into a mere object of our awareness, so that we can talk about him but cannot listen to him, live by him, obey him, or love him.

Today the church finds itself too far gone in ease and comfort to be roused by the mystery of the Cross. It lives in a world too reasonable to expect the Resurrection, too sensible to live in hope of something to come. We have the feeling that the inauguration of the kingdom is at hand for us, though not yet apparent. So we clean the house and set the table before the

invitation is actually sent out. In the end we may find ourselves in for a terrible surprise: We will find that the seats have
already been reserved for those who are travelling hopefully
through the darkness of this world. (. . .)

71

To his parents

September 14
(. . .) Here the unbroken calm of prison life goes on as usual.
The only news is that A. has been freed. I read in the newspaper that the Dominican prior of Montreal, Father Demarais,
will come to Brazil to observe our trial as representative of our
father general. (. . .) He's the author of a best seller called
Optimism Pills. I hope he brings some for us too.

Although we're neither pessimists nor optimists, prison is a
degrading place for a human being. Not for Christians, who
know that one way or another we must pass through such a
trial. But as an institution, prison is abominable. It is such a
contradiction of the outside world that it ends by teaching you
many things, about freedom in particular.

Above all, prison makes you examine your life, thoughts,
scale of values, and many things that outward freedom does
not always teach. It is a darkness in which many things are
glimpsed and you can judge your own worth.

Meanwhile we wait for them to decide our fate. There are
many people all over the world in a similar situation, so there is
no sense in feeling that we have a monopoly on suffering. Our
suffering is a symptom of the age in which we live. Time will
pass, and so will our suffering. It's a matter of patience and
hope. Feeling certain that this period of gestation will bear
fruit, I pray that you be inspired with the same faith that
animated Abraham and Sarah in the matter of their son (see
Genesis 12ff.).

72

October 11

(. . .) I've been making the rounds of São Paulo prisons. I've spent almost twenty days as an involuntary hermit in the prison attached to the cavalry division of the military police. The experience was both profitable and terrible. There wasn't much to do. Or rather there was absolutely nothing to do. I managed to devote myself more intensely to prayer. The days were long, as they always are when you await the unknown. I woke to the braying of bugles, paced the narrow cell with short steps, and said my morning prayers. I had some black coffee with bread and butter, then went back to pacing. Then I sat down on my bunk and propped my feet on the opposite wall. To divert myself I would sing whatever snatches of songs I knew, make up others, conjure up past incidents and mentally retouch them. Old times would spring to mind with the immediacy and clarity of a photograph. At night there was a different sort of diversion, but it was hardly pleasant: I would observe the comings and goings of the cockroaches, who seemed well fed for a place where food is scarce. I kept trying to get them off the bunk, because there was only room for me on it.

After a week there, I got my own copy of the New Testament. I gave myself up to reading it avidly, trying to memorize the passages most relevant to my position. I read the four Gospels, learned Saint Paul's itineraries, and was deeply impressed by the realism and topicality of the Apocalypse. I came to realize that I was at my proper post. The monotony was then broken by a visit from an official, the most humane and sensitive one that I have met in my tour of prisons. It was a moment of contact, catharsis, and relief.

Life has afforded me the opportunity to undergo all these experiences. I do what I can to profit from them, to extract understanding from them, and to grow in my vocation as a Christian. In my heart of hearts I feel great joy, not because I am a prisoner but because I can see how free I still am (. . .).

73

To the Dominican community in São Paulo

November 3

Dear Friends, I have learned that you were satisfied with my depositions in court. I believe that I made myself clear, and that I aptly expounded my position as a Christian and as a religious. I came back to prison greatly relieved, as one would be when a long-dreaded exam is finally over. But the greatest joy of all was the release of R. and A. I learned that you had a fine celebration in the monastery.

Now our cell is emptier. There are five Dominicans here, along with a Blessed Sacrament father who was sentenced to fourteen months for a sermon he preached in a small town in the interior of São Paulo state.

Right now we are completely isolated from the other prisoners. Our cells, visiting schedules, and recreation periods are completely separate. Little by little we are adjusting the cell to our needs as best we can. The main thing is that we now have the minimum we need to get some studying done. From the prison authorities we managed to get some crude bookcases and a table. Now all we need is more lighting, because right now we really cannot see well at night (. . .).

Today we were visited by a Dominican bishop, Tomas Balduino of Goias. The new archbishop of São Paulo, Evaristo Arns, came to see us the day after his appointment. We had listened to his inaugural address on the radio, and we liked his firm and direct style very much. I have increasing confidence in the action of the Holy Spirit within the church. He blows where he wills and when we least expect him, but always at the right moment. (. . .)

On November 9 I will have spent a whole year in prison, perhaps the richest and most surprising year of my life, or at least the one I have lived most intensely (. . .).

74

To another religious community

November 9

(. . .) I received your letters expressing your approval of our court depositions. The preliminary questioning really went well. We were not afraid to speak the truth or to point out that the Christian spirit, compelled by love, far surpasses anything that the human mind has invented to preserve private interests that are not always identical with the common good.

If I have made a mistake in explaining my conduct, it is the same error as the one in the parable of the good Samaritan. He did not ask the man lying in the road if he was good or bad, if he had been beaten while doing good or attempting a crime. Jesus says only that there was a wounded man lying in the road in need of help. The Samaritan helped him without asking questions about his past, his intentions, or his motives. He picked him up, brought him to an inn, and footed the bill for his recovery and care.

The point of the parable is summed up nicely in an old proverb: *"Faze o bem, sem olher a quem"* "Good you should do, no matter for who." (. . .)

75

To his parents

November 15

Dearest Mom and Dad, after a year in prison we have received the body of Our Lord in Communion for the first time in our cell. Last Thursday the chaplain of the military police celebrated Mass here and left us some consecrated wafers. He's a good guy who gave us a lot of support when we were in isolation in the barracks. Now every evening after our traditional card game we recite the Psalms and receive Communion.

Wednesday we saw Father Domingos[48] again, to our great joy. He brought us greetings and best wishes from the whole Dominican family in Europe, and a letter from our father general assuring us that we are still his sons and containing a beautiful photograph of a thirteenth-century stone carving of Saint Dominic. On the photograph are the famous words of Dominic's great friend and disciple, Jordan of Saxony: "Dominic revealed himself to all, by word and deed, as a man of the gospel." We each got a copy inscribed with our name and the blessing of father general.

It seems that there's a lot of sympathy for us in Rome. Father Domingos had expressed a wish to see the pope, but he wasn't optimistic about its being granted. Within twenty-four hours, he received a letter notifying him that he had been granted an audience for the following day. It is rare for the pope to grant an audience so quickly. When Father Domingos entered his presence, Paul VI made as if to rise and embrace him, but protocol did not permit that. He said that he was following our case closely and had advised the nuncio to help us in any way we needed. He said that he stood by us in our sufferings and sent us his blessing. At the end of the audience he gave Father Domingos a little gift for us as a token of his affection: a beautiful little box with a cross made of olive wood that grew in Jerusalem. Ordinarily Paul VI gives a gift of rosary beads to visitors (Charles De Gaulle was buried with his hands crossed beneath his). This extraordinary gift to us reveals his affection. You may recall that some time ago we sent the pope a little wooden cross with our names carved into it that we had made here in prison. Well, it seems that he did receive our gift.

Father Domingos also visited three Dominican contemplative monasteries in France. All three were deeply interested in our case and sent us various little mementos, and they pray for us. One cloister, the one in Blagnac, is rather out of the ordinary: It accepts sick and infirm people so that they too can dedicate themselves to the religious life. There is a young nun there who entered after a terrible automobile accident. She has already gone through several operations that she was not expected to survive. After hearing Father Domingos preach, she submitted a petition to her mother superior. Her note was simple, personal, and private, but the mother superior gave it to Father Domingos, and it ended up in our hands. I was deeply moved when I read it: "Dear Mother Superior, if you wish, you may tell Father Domingos that I am offering up my sufferings to the Lord for our brothers in prison. God knows how much I suffer! In particular, I am offering up my next operation, in which I will try to be more courageous, more faithful, and more religious with the aim of helping our brothers." It was signed "Sister Marike." We wrote to her.

The more we are forced to live in isolation, the more we feel part of a huge family that knows no boundaries of language, culture, or nationality (. . .).

76

To Sister Marike, a French nun

November 15

Dear Sister, the words you wrote so pointedly have reached us through your mother superior. They have pierced to the depths of this prison where we have spent the last year for the sake of Christ's gospel. Your words are here before us, and they make us weep. Suffering is the point of encounter for Christians because it is a proclamation of the Resurrection. Now that we are aware of your sufferings, we know that the Lord has already transformed them into grace for us. Your letter makes us feel a renewal of our conversion in intimacy with our crucified Lord. He has prepared a banquet, and by his grace we prisoners have been invited. There at the table we have met you, in the place of honor, joyous and radiant. You have asked to be "more courageous, more faithful, and more religious"; that you are. Today we too make the same request as we think of you, for we are united by faith, hope, and love. We know that neither lack of freedom in the world nor lack of bodily health can prevent us from growing in the freedom of the Spirit or the life of God. Everything is grace. The road to the Resurrection passes through prison corridors and hospital operating rooms. In great friendship,

Carlos Alberto (Betto) Christo, O.P.
Yves Lesbaupin, O.P.
Fernando de Brito, O.P.
Helio Soares do Amaral, S.S.S.
Giorgio Callegari, O.P.
Tito de Alencar de Lima, O.P.

77

To a religious community[49]

November 15
Feast of St. Albert the Great

Dear Dominican Sisters, Father Domingos has brought us a little bit of your life. We are grateful for your news and your cards. We are glad to know that people in a little corner of Europe are praying for us and sharing our sufferings.

We too live in a cloister where Christ is present, barred and guarded by armed soldiers. Our life here is simple, filled with the unforeseen and with hope. We are five Dominicans and a Blessed Sacrament father. Roberto was released on October 28. We sleep in our cell, as well as study, pray, and cook here. All of us have learned to cook. It is not only a necessity but also a pastime. We give our imaginations rein by inventing dishes that can be found only on our menu.

Every evening we recite the Psalms together, and our chanting rings through the corridor of the prison. We are prohibited from celebrating Mass, but we can now receive Communion because the chaplain has left us some consecrated wafers. We are allowed outside our cells three hours a week, and we can have visitors every two weeks. Our cell is rectangular, small, and crude with a high, barred window at the back. Through the bars we can see the sky and experience a sense of the infinite and of the certainty that our spirits know no bounds.

We thank you very much for your prayers. For you we offer

up our sufferings in Christ, who was also imprisoned and condemned. We know that all this is part of God's design and can be found at the very origins of the church. Unfortunately, we are not always capable of echoing the "fiat" that Mary taught us, but a profound joy pervades our lives. We praise the Lord who has deemed us worthy to be in prison, for here there are many who have been invited to his banquet.

We are bound to your convent and to each of you by the strong bonds of sanctifying grace. In great friendship,

> Carlos Alberto (Betto) Christo, O.P.
> Yves Lesbaupin, O.P.
> Helio Soares do Amaral, S.S.S.
> Giorgio M. Callegari, O.P.
> Fernando de Brito, O.P.
> Tito de Alencar de Lima, O.P.

78

To another religious community

November 19

(. . .) We cannot complain of the church, which has given us its support. We know that many religious communities in Europe are praying for us. Even at Lourdes pilgrims have prayed for us. This makes us more keenly aware of the communion of saints, more a part of the invisible but real church. One small part of this church is here behind bars, but it also extends wherever human beings are suffering and thus taking part in the redemption of the world. It includes those who have fallen by the wayside, who are poor. The kingdom is growing in their hearts, though they may not know it, or may perceive it only dimly. It summons us to a deeper sense of responsibility.

On the outside, in another sector, we built a church of flowering gardens, erudite sermons, and a guaranteed number of baptisms. But here we find people who are living the mystery of the crucified Christ in a continuing augury of the Resurrection. Their suffering bodies are the temple, their spilt blood is the baptism, their existential communion with Christ is the Eucharist. The church on the "outside" cannot know this human reality theoretically. Only by real life practice can its manifold riches be known. But it is not easy to cross the boundary line between theory and practice. The church in prison sends you a big hug.

79

To Pedro

Dear Friend, in your last letter you mentioned how difficult it is to establish a dialogue with the poor because their language is nearly incomprehensible to the cleric. The difficulty is of our own making. We have dissociated ourselves from the normal concerns of most people's lives under the pretext of thus becoming available for preaching the gospel. Many of us come from working-class families, and more than one cardinal has come from peasant stock. Our early entry into the seminary tears us away from our native environments and our families and offers us a way of life that represents a step up on the social scale. Our classical education alters our way of thinking and our vocabulary. The long training period in the cloister removes us from the real problems that affect the lives of everyone except the clergy and the rich. Is it possible at this point to build a bridge between our world and the world outside our ecclesiastical institutions? Is it possible to alter our point of view and our way of life?

When Pius XI stated that the church had lost the working class, he meant that the church had become so bourgeois that it had lost a feeling for the poor. As a result, the worker-priest experiment came into being. I think the problem will be solved not by priests becoming workers but only when we get workers as priests, when workers can join our ranks without betraying their origins. To reach that point, however, we will have to break down many barriers, put an end to many taboos, and move from doctrinal speculation to Christian experience. What good is preaching without witness?

What worries me is that this renewal will not come about by our choice and personal initiative but will be forced on us by circumstances. The fact is that these circumstances are already becoming apparent, exerting pressure on us, and forcing us to adopt new patterns of behavior.

As you know, we are not allowed to receive the sacraments here. Yet never in my life have I experienced the sacraments so vitally as I have here. I think our circumstances have forced us to interiorize the spirit of the gospel as never before. (All you need is the specter of death before your eyes!) The totality of prison becomes a great channel of divine life. And how visible a sign it is!

Only the term *kenosis* can convey all that we are undergoing, for we have come to the point where all values exist solely within us. We accept our existence as a stripping away of all externals, for we have no idea when we will get out of here or what our life will be like. The only certain thing is that this episode in our lives places us in the context of Christ.

Now I can understand what my parish priest in Rio meant by saying: "The poor, by the very fact of being poor, attain to a union with Christ as intimate and real as that of the mystic." He also used to say that the real presence of Christ could be found in the sacraments and in the poor. That is true, I think. It is easier for people to meet Christ and recognize him when their living conditions resemble his.

The hard thing is to get to this theological "reduction" that puts us on Christ's level. We are imprinted with the Hellenic conception of God and have lost sight of the reality of him who is the very negation of that conception: Jesus Christ. Our religious reference point is more the idea of God than the life of the poor and persecuted Jesus. So we have lost the Semitic, biblical, historical, and eschatological dimension of Christian life.

Thanks for the texts you sent. Our fellow prisoners' interest in Christianity is striking. The material you sent is a great help. (. . .)

115

80

To his brother Luiz Fernando

November 29

(. . .) Joy, Joy, Joy! You need a lot of courage to be happy in the midst of so much suffering. You need strength. What can we do but believe in ourselves as the Lord taught us to do? We must see the human adventure through to the end without hesitating or complaining.

I try to find this joy within myself and draw it out so as to give a little of it to those who inhabit the other cold and gloomy cells in pavillion 2. It's a dreadful building, old as the tragedy of the human condition. On the ground floor are those who have been invited to the Lord's banquet, one or two hundred people who live by the law of the jungle. At night they cry their bitterness to the wind, beating out the rhythm on tin cans. They sing their desperation and their impotence in the face of the world and of life. They endure in silence an existence unknown to the rest of the world. They are the alienated ones, the people who stand on street corners and make passersby afraid.

On the upper floor are a hundred or so prisoners who have been arrested and charged under the government's security laws. They are laid out in the cells like so many packages in a huge refrigerator. We, half a dozen Christians, are kept in the rear, isolated from the other prisoners. We cannot talk to the other prisoners, but now the prison chaplain is permitted to bring us the body of our risen Lord, who alone can know whether we are worthy of it or not. I know the effort it costs me not to hate. . . . This is no mere difference of opinion. We live in history, and the future will show who was right. The future will judge imprisonment to be as abominable as torture and the Inquisition.

I know just how much despair waits in ambush behind these walls. Like unshed tears, it corrodes the heart, even the hearts of the young. Not all of us have the wisdom or strength to resist the situation in which we find ourselves. Not everyone manages to see in the dark. To those who put you in prison, you are just another face. To you who are put in prison, this is your whole life.

Facing our cell there is a cell full of common prisoners —bank robbers. One of them is twenty-four years old and has been sentenced to the same number of years in prison. Does that strike you as a reasonable period for rehabilitating a person? Does he need that much time to make a new decision about life? Can he do it under these conditions, locked in a cage and left to his own devices?

We must be happy and love with all our strength to keep hatred and despair from taking possession of us. We must stay calm, or the vast corridor that runs the length of the prison will end by devouring us. We must remain patient, or the rattling of keys that are not ours will make us deaf. We must have trust and confidence.

Human existence is radically transcendent. Only this transcendence, felt even by those who do not believe, keeps you from commiting suicide.

Pray for us.

81

To Pedro

December 4

Dear Friend, we read your letter together yesterday evening, after reciting the Psalms and before receiving Holy Communion. What you say coincides with what we are thinking here in the darkness of this world. I would like to write you my opinions on some of the most hotly debated issues in the church today.

First of all, I agree with Bishop Fragoso's[50] remarks on the institutional church: "In *this* church we will reach renewal and salvation. Because *this* church is us." There is no heavenly church, no papal church, no church hovering above humankind like an intangible, venerable image. If the church has gone wrong, it is we who have gone wrong. If the church reflects the authentic image of Jesus Christ, then it is we who are letting ourselves be led by the Spirit. Quitting the church is as impossible as quitting ourselves. If the institution is ponderous, backward, and rusted, it is we who have made it so. And we can also make it light, flexible, and forward looking.

The church is the great responsibility that Christ entrusted to us. It is not identical with him, but it is identical with us. It was founded by Christ, but it is also the work of human beings. We can repudiate it and prostitute it, or we can purify and sanctify it. We can even dismember it. But the church is us; it is ours; and it is truly the church only if it is consistent with the gospel. We do not have a separate church for each aspect of life: the church of leisure, the church of social work, and so forth. We have only one church, the church of faith in God's word. Those who wish to renew the church "from outside" may be able to renew themselves, but never the church. If church renewal "from inside" is difficult, that is because we have neither the courage to speak nor the humility to listen because the seminary taught us that the bishop has a monopoly on truth; but the bishop cannot always distinguish between his personal truth and the truth of the gospel. The two truths do not always coincide.

When I was arrested in Porto Alegre, I heard that someone in the episcopate regarded me with misgivings. But I had prayerfully scrutinized all my attitudes, declining to commit a sin of omission. I did not become disheartened. Today the pastor of Porto Alegre came to break bread with us in our cell. But what if things had turned out differently? What if I had been refused orders and "furloughed" from my religious family? I asked myself these questions. I thought about the silence imposed on men like Congar, De Lubac, and Teilhard de Chardin, and how they kept faith nonetheless. Their faith assured them of hope. If the Lord has brought me to prison, where I never would have chosen to go, he can bring me elsewhere. There are many ways to serve him and many roads to redemption—even outside the institution of the church.

You write: "A growing number are leaving." That is true,

particularly among the clergy. There are many who are tired of being priests, who feel empty within, who are attracted by the delights and possibilities of lay life. In part this is the fault of the structures that we have fashioned, adorned, and canonized, and that we now wish to tear down. It is not the fault of those who pull out. They are leaving to be more authentically themselves, to live more realistically, to look for what they cannot find within the church. Their departure is a challenge to those of us who remain.

I do not mean to say that they are dissatisfied with the enduring institution of the church as such. I think that their dissatisfaction has to do with the structures of the institution which have only transitory worth. Such things as seminaries, religious constitutions, discipline, canon law, the curia, the college of cardinals, and parishes are part of this structure and have no eternal value. The church came into existence without them, and it can live without them. Crisis occurs when we absolutize these structural elements and then, when they are challenged, react as though a vital part of the church is being torn away—as though the very essence of the church is being mutilated. But Christ founded his church with twelve poor, uneducated men. We will ruin it if we do not remember its origins. Most of the priests who leave are abandoning the structures, not the church as an institution. Many of them would still like to exercise their priestly ministry—within the framework of *new structures.* But they don't have the patience to wait out the long gestation period necessary to change a church by now embedded in seventeen centuries of tradition.

Unfortunately their contributions to society from outside the church often fall short of expectation. Frequently they are so deeply involved with their own personal problems that they can see nothing beyond their new domestic lives. The most serious danger for those who leave the priesthood is the eventual loss of faith. It is serious for us who do not provide convincing witness. It is scandalous that people lose their faith within our seminaries. It means that our Christian life is sluggish, individualistic, moralistic, and short of courage and risk and daring. It means that our seminaries turn out priests, preachers, philosophers, and theologians—but how many of them are Christians? How many of them would be able to risk their lives for the faith?

I know several priests who left to get married. Here we have the whole problem of celibacy. In my opinion we must pay much greater attention to the problem of training people for celibacy. We consider celibacy a charism whose value lies in making possible our total service to the kingdom of God and in bearing witness to its eschatological fulfillment. But we must not forget that this charism has to develop, that our awareness of this fulfillment must mature over time. As things now stand, the assumption is that every priest must have a vocation to celibacy. So it is most important that we train people in such a way that our celibates do not become neurotic, maladjusted people whose feelings of unease towards the sensual world produce conflict and disillusionment. At present, however, it is assumed in our seminaries that every candidate for the priesthood is a potential celibate. To protect this charism, obstacles are put in the way of any and all contact with the sensual world, in particular with women. It is worse when the seminarian has not had any adolescence, when he has been a seminarian since the age of eleven, plucked too young from the bosom of his family and from natural friendships and tossed into the artificial and inhuman setting of some minor seminary. At the age of thirty, such a person is still acting like a teenager.

Another serious matter is the illusion that we try to impose on the candidate: that love of God will be a substitute for human love. That is a lie. Celibacy is a real renunciation. The void remains, and nothing mystical fills it up. Saint Teresa of Avila speaks of this void. She says that it is there that we learn how much we are capable of loving and how much we are capable of giving up for the sake of love. In this void we learn to what extent we are human and masculine, capable of loving a woman and making her happy. One who doubts his sexuality will suffer greatly, because asexuality is an abnormality. A priest can find self-fulfillment in celibacy only if he is fully conscious of his masculinity.

The great value of this charism consists in liberating us for service and above all in bearing witness to the greatness of the faith. I don't think an asexual priest can bear valid witness to his celibacy. By the way, every prison inmate is a celibate by force of circumstances. Many inmates have said to me: "I would never have thought it possible, but now I understand through personal experience how you priests can live without women."

A man's emotional maturity does not depend on matrimony, but the fact remains that many clerics are emotionally immature. The explanation lies in their defective, rationalistic training that is too dissociated from real life. This is why we have so many intelligent and educated priests whose naiveté and insecurity are painful to see. And this is also why I feel that no one should enter a seminary before the age of twenty. It will be a great day when we celibate priests can live side by side with married priests. (. . .)

82

December 6

(. . .) We must interpret in the present God's will for the future, using our awareness of the community in history and our memory of the past. You indicate to me how the Bible is relevant today and the extent to which it provides us with an empirico-theological means of analyzing the present and the future in the light of faith. Your observations demythologize the Bible so that it is no longer a book of magic accessible only to experts. Quite the contrary, the Bible is God's loving colloquy with human beings in history. As you see it, any workingman can understand the word of God and seek in it a guide to conduct.

I have the feeling that all our theology is too erudite. We speak a language inaccessible to the man in the street, who remains satisfied with superstitions, syncretism, and magic. How can we make him understand the meaning of religion stripped of dreamy sentimentalism? How can we make him develop an attitude toward life that is consciously based on Jesus Christ? The spirituality we convey is individualistic, disembodied, and neutral. It is a spirituality of submission and resignation that turns people into slaves or bourgeoisie. It is not a socially conscious spirituality—not an incarnate, bold, committed, risk-taking spirituality of courage and redeeming faith.

Hence the attitude of the Christian in the Western world is frequently passive, fatalistic, submissive to anything that smacks of tradition, law and order, prestige, and stability. Faith does not evoke a critical attitude. Religion is a kind of anesthetic to dull the sufferings of life, a consolation in misfortune, in short, an opiate. Christians settle down in a church in which they are assured of salvation and promised a reward hereafter. Their religious concern is to lead honest and well-regulated lives according to the false, opportunistic precepts of bourgeois society and culture. Good Christians are the good citizens, the ones who dispute nothing, challenge nothing, question nothing, protest nothing, claim nothing, subvert nothing. Sin for them is a purely individual phenomenon. God is a white God, a colonizing, land-owning, governing God—the God of the European who hoists the banner of liberty, equality, and fraternity and then uses it to shaft the peoples of Asia, Africa, and Latin America.

It will take more than an act of contrition to wipe away our sins from history. Our debt is still great. The crimes continue, and we preach peace and lack courage to denounce the assassins or to side with the victims. For us everything becomes "a delicate matter" requiring "prudence." Isn't prudence the church's greatest sin, the cause of all its sins of omission? This is one of the questions for whose answer we must look into the Bible. (. . .)

83

(. . .) Nothing is so attractive to a human being as freedom. Even animals and plants grow toward the light. Even a condemned man, whose freedom depends on serving out his prison sentence, will still count off the days bringing him closer to freedom. A boy who had served three years in prison told me that the worst time of all was the last year. It was then that he suffered most, for it passed so slowly. Every passing day was like the end of a great battle that would have to be fought over and over again until the war was finally over. A prisoner sentenced for an indefinite period suffers less because he can always hope that his imprisonment will be brief, although he may suffer more if he cannot be patient in the face of uncertainty.

In any case freedom exerts an irresistible magnetism on everyone. To be free, to be able to walk about at will, to be alone (which is impossible in a crowded prison), to plan for the future: All that is a dream right now. Since I don't even know when the future will arrive, I can only wait and regard my present situation as normal. I must create a certain rhythm of life here in prison, trying to improve myself despite the limitations. I must not give way to laziness, depression, or illusion.

Illusions weigh heavy in prison! Often you meet a prisoner doomed to a long stretch who nevertheless insists that, for quite inexplicable reasons, he knows he is getting out at the end of the month or the year. Imagination takes over; you begin to perform all sorts of mental acrobatics and end up crediting your wishful thinking more than your actual legal situation. From one newspaper article a prisoner will draw a thousand deductions and from them convince himself that he is about to be freed. It happens often here, and it is an awful thing to see.

Every now and then such a person regains his senses and realizes that his imagination has run riot. Then he gives way to confusion and depression, to a sense of failure, and to rebelliousness. But the madness is cyclical, and soon he falls prey to his imaginings again. They tranquilize him and temporarily lessen his pain, although his wound remains.

When you run into such an individual, it is useless to point out to him that he is mistaken. You must resign yourself to listen to him, pretend to agree with his reasoning, and share his harmless euphoria. Trying to contradict him would be like kicking in a child's sandcastle at the beach. (. . .)

84

To his parents

December 11

(. . .) I have so much to say, but my powers of expression are as limited as the space in this cell. It's hard to think in a situation in which the unforeseen can happen at any moment. You exist in a state of absolute uncertainty. Everything is waiting, tension, surprise. There is no end in sight, nothing we can count on. Destiny becomes for us either a palpable presence or a matter of total indifference.

This is the third kidnapping of a diplomat[51] that has reverberated through this prison since I've been here. It's curious that you never really get used to an event like this. It always has a tremendous impact on your unconscious. Even a prisoner who is sure that his name will not be selected finds it hard to disregard the possibility of being unexpectedly free. He shares the sense of expectancy that grips everyone. At every bit of news, every step of the negotiations, he feels as if his life is riding on a throw of the dice. There is little basis for predicting what will happen. You only know, for example, that those who will be freed will probably be prisoners charged with offenses carrying long sentences. But there are many surprises.

I don't see why the groups who carry out these kidnappings should have any interest in me. The only organization to which I belong is the church. The case of Mother Maurina[52] can be explained, I think, by the fact that she is a nun, the only woman arrested on such grounds in the West. Freeing her was designed to have political repercussions. Too many priests and religious have been arrested in too many places for us to be newsworthy.

What gets to us is not so much the possibility of personal liberation as the psychosis, the uncontrollable sense of expectation created among the prisoners at these times. In short it is the imminence of freedom for a whole group of people who must otherwise remain in prison for a long time. (. . .)

85

To Pedro

December 18

(. . .) Everything that society banishes from its midst ends up here. It's like a giant sewer into which refuse drains on its way to the ocean that is freedom. Living in a sewer is an indescribable experience. Here all sorts of castoffs meet, both the bad and the good. Each cell is one tank in the great dam that is prison. We live here together with the moles and cockroaches that breed under the city. We smell of our lack of freedom, almost unbearably. Above us the rest of the city goes on as usual, chewing, digesting, and excreting what it produces. Through these sad and narrow tunnels of cement and iron run people's dreams, ideals, blood, hopes, and unalterable faith that the water of the ocean is not far away. One day we will get there, and then the desert will bloom and the oases will dry up.

Here underground great things are happening. There are seeds germinating, a stream of water wearing away the rock, life asserting itself. Here lie the roots that will flower in the spring. It is underground that we find gold and silver and the roots of ancient oak trees. It is here that everything is born, blossoms, and grows toward the sunlight. From the earth comes power, nourishment, richness, and security; but since the sun is above, everything reaches ineluctably toward the light. Ascent is the natural motion of everything that exists.

Life in the darkness of this world teaches us to see things differently. It makes us morose as cockroaches, terrible as plague-bearing rats. It obliterates many of our former values, and makes us friends of the dark—which conceals what should be laid bare. We learn to feel our way, to see in the dark, to tell things by their smells. We know how to walk through potholes and puddles. Our only light against the darkness is the light of the Holy Spirit. We hear voices and can't tell where they come from, but they don't sound incoherent. Someone says, "This way!" Another cries out, "That way!" Holding each other's hands, we look for the way out of the darkness. Sometimes we are dashed against the walls and lose contact with each other. Sometimes the silence is broken by outbursts of mocking laughter or convulsive weeping. We fall, and love stops the bleeding of our wounds. Only hatred causes them to hemorrhage, although salvation may require a complete transfusion.

After a while, we become familiar with the mysteries of the darkness. We lose our fear, our need for security and consolation, our attachment to what the darkness has rendered invisible. We also lose our absolute certainties, our dogmatic truths, our interest in defending perfection, order, and purity. We come to believe in sin, anguish, need, uncertainty, and risk. We cling to the refuse that thickens on the walls, finding acceptance and repose in it. It is useless to be holy, pacifist, meek, resigned, and good, and we no longer are any of these things. We are pariahs, criminals, dissenters—banished, oppressed, and alienated: the wretched of the earth. If we are granted a little more life, it is because we are sure of this now.

But it is in all this that we find salvation. We identify with one who was born in a stable and died on the cross. We bear in our own flesh the stigmata of sorrow and suffering. Our faces are drenched with tears, but our hearts go on beating. Their beating rouses us. It keeps our blood moving and quickens our lives. Ill treated and in rags, we hear the voice of him who bids us to the banquet where the chalice of his blood will slake our present thirst. The more we try to control our feelings of expectation, the keener they become.

126

This is our path. It leads to liberation. It winds, but it never turns back. To turn back is to betray, to be afraid. We have passed the point of no return. We cannot look back. We can only go on. (. . .)

86

To his family

December 25

Dear Ones, it's Christmas night in prison. It brings back our childhood, midnight mass and gift-giving, the feast of meat and wine. I feel like writing a poem, but I know I'm not a poet. Tonight I feel very close to you. I feel freedom and tremendous joy that has been forged out of suffering, like the water that comes flowing from the rocks.

Today a contagious joy infects our prison. Clearly all of us here feel tremendous longing for those we love who are "outside." But it is also clear that even here, by living together so long and so intimately, we prisoners have become a family. In each of us who hunger and thirst for justice, peace, and liberty, he who embodies these ideals is being reborn: the infant Jesus.

The best gift of all was the release of Giorgio. He went off like a kid on the first morning of summer vacation. Radiant with happiness, he was reborn into the world. Now there are four of us in cell 17, and we may be reduced to three. Tito is among those whose release is demanded in exchange for the Swiss ambassador.[53]

Christmas night in prison. The guards came to wish us a Merry Christmas, and we wished them the same. Shortly before midnight we celebrated our liturgy. We chanted the Gloria, meditated on the Nativity according to St. Luke, sang the Magnificat, and recited the Psalms. Our Christmas dinner consisted of meat sandwiches on rolls, eggs, and tomatoes. For dessert we had a box of chocolates, which were gotten past the authorities with some difficulty because they have a little bit of liquor in them.

Now the whole prison is singing, as if our song alone, happy and free, must sound throughout the world. The women are singing over in their section, and we applaud. Bars and walls cannot imprison voices; they burst forth from hearts filled with friendship and love and united by a shared hope. On the floor below the nonpolitical prisoners are singing too. They beat out the *batuque*—the rhythm of the slums—on cans and boxes. Everyone here knows that it's Christmas, that someone is being reborn. And with our song we testify that we too have been reborn to fight for a world without tears, hatred, or oppression.

It's quite something to see these young faces pressed against the bars and singing their love. Unforgettable. It's not a sight for our judges, or the public prosecutor, or the police who arrested us. They would find the beauty of this night intolerable. Torturers fear a smile, even a weak one.

The acoustics of the prison corridor are very good. The whole place seems to be vibrating, as if everything that's meant by living free were blowing on the gentle wind of this summer night.[54] We can feel it because we are prisoners for the sake of other people's freedom.

In front of our cell stands a huge black man with a powerful voice, directing the singing. He is the top singer in this prison. He spends his days shouting from his cell: "Do you mean to say that besides being a prisoner I must put up with promiscuity? Let me out of here; I know your kind very well." He was arrested this year and probably won't get out for twenty years. Now he is telling us to get to *la* because our *re* is falling flat. (. . .)

This is another world. Many things cannot be told now. But I will remember it all forever. We will never be free of this experience, especially because it has taught us so much.

I hope that you are as happy as we are. Especially tonight, the bonds of faith bring us together. May our Father grant you all the best for the new year.

87

To his brothers and sisters

December 26

(. . .) Last Wednesday the Military Tribunal reviewed the petition for freedom on bail and house arrest that had been presented by our defense attorney, Mario Simas. The answer was no. The decisive factor in the eyes of the public prosecutor was the recent terrible fire at the Volkswagen plant in São Paulo. It must have been the work of terrorists, and it cost thirty lives and left many injured. I cannot figure out the relationship between that fire and our petition. It must be astrological, especially since the true cause of the blaze has not yet been ascertained.

All the same I must confess that the outcome is all right with me. I don't like the idea of house arrest, even in a monastery or episcopal residence. It's a matter of principle. I don't think I should contribute to turning a church into a prison or making a bishop into a jailer. The church's mission is to proclaim freedom, not to help suppress it. The church is a gift from God. Out of love of freedom and respect for this gift, I prefer to remain in the hands of those *who force me* to be a prisoner. I prefer to stay here. The church cannot and must not ever become a branch of the Brazilian prison system. There can be no fence-sitting in matters of principle. The easiest way is not always the right way. Hence I feel a certain relief at the decision of those who are my de jure and de facto jailers not to grant me house arrest.

88

To a religious community[55]

December 27

(. . .) I am deeply attached to the monastic life. I have always defended it, because I know that in the monastery one leads a committed life, a committed, contemplative life. And this contemplation is not unmindful of the Resurrection as the consummation of God's incarnation in history. We reach heaven via the streets of earth and God through encounters with other people. This witness to this faith, received in the monastery, has kept me from lapsing at various times into disdain for the contemplative life. I have always kept it in mind, and I have always felt a secret attraction for that way of life.

Insofar as the active life is concerned, the Lord has helped me to surmount obstacles that seemed insurmountable. My paths have always been turbulent and dangerous. Today I accept all that as part of my vocation. The Lord has called me through the voices of unbelievers. He has brought me to the very center of life in the world—to prison. He has cast me into the darkness of this world and this life. There, where I once thought only malice, indifference, and sin existed, I have found grace, fidelity, love, and hope. Christ's missioners may well be inclined not to stick their necks out; they may well prefer to keep close to the safety of parish and cloister, of catechism class and the dinner tables of the bourgeoisie, where the priest is an honored guest. But Christ stuck his neck out. He wasn't afraid to be tempted, vilified, and cursed, or to be friend to prostitutes and sinners. It didn't bother him to be called drunkard, glutton, law-breaker, and flouter of tradition. Christ went where we haven't the courage to go. While we look for him in the temple, he is in a stable. While we look for him among priests, he is among sinners. While we look for him among the free, he is a prisoner. While we look for him in glory, he is bleeding on the cross. It is we who have created distinctions, dividing the world into good people and bad. We think that God is bound by our ideas and preconceptions and formulations; but time and time again he sits on our doorsteps and asks for a slice of bread. . . .

I too was brought up in a milieu much given to expressing disdain for the poor, the blacks—whomever we considered the scum of the earth. Now I find myself among such people. Thrown into a narrow, stinking cell where the air reeks of sweat, I find myself surrounded by criminals—gangsters, murderers, thieves, child-molesters—people I would be afraid to run into on the street at night. And in my petit-bourgeois arrogance I think: "I must bring Christ to these people. I must improve them." But what do I discover? I discover that it is they who are revealing the true image of Christ to me. They stand alongside the crucified Christ and join him in accomplishing our redemption. I am ashamed of myself. I no longer know what to say. I only know that I must lay myself open to receive God's gift, to understand, like these people whom I call "the guests at Christ's banquet."

Of one thing I am certain: They are saved. Their thefts and murders are not their fault but ours. Why? Because we have not been wise enough to respect the rights of our neighbor. Because we have been selfish, greedy, and rich. Because we have drawn our blinds to shut out the sight of their slums. Because we have consented to the division between rich and poor. Because we have looked on these people with suspicion, disgust, and fear. They are poor, lowly, rejected, and condemned—like Christ. They are the living image of the Lord. (. . .)

89

To Sister Stella, a Brazilian contemplative nun

December 27

(. . .) I'm sure you weren't expecting a letter from me. But I suddenly felt the urge to write you, God knows why. It's daybreak, the time when I pray, meditate, and write. A prisoner's time is not rigidly scheduled. Today for example we ate our midday meal at three in the afternoon (mashed potatoes). Sometimes we have supper at four in the morning. Here we are at least free to ignore the clock, a freedom almost impossible on the outside.

I have many reasons for wanting to dialogue with you. It was eleven years ago that I first tramped up the stone path leading to your convent. It was carnival time, and I was making a retreat with a Catholic Action group in your chaplain's quarters. I visted the convent faithfully from 1959 to 1962. There I came to know Father M., who seemed to me poles apart from us, incapable of looking without suspicion upon the Catholic Action movement. That was the time when we were discovering the social dimension of the Christian message. A person with fond memories of the movement for liturgical renewal[56] had a hard time feeling kindly toward all the social agitation that, following Vatican II, became the preoccupation and mission of the whole church. Then I made friends with Father A., a plain man forged in the harsh and humble school of missionary work among the Indians. I wonder where he is today.

In those days I became friendly with a boy who used to serve Mass every day at the convent. I would jump out of bed every morning at the sound of his motorbike turning the corner of our street. We would climb the hill for Mass in the poor and somber chapel of the convent. Its walls were faced only with brick, and from the other side of the broad wooden grating we could hear the sweet and moving chanting of the nuns. Then we would have coffee in the little parlor. What a beautiful time it was! (. . .)

Now I'll talk a little about myself. There are four of us Dominicans in this cell, which is no bigger than the parlor of your convent. We get out only twice a week, for an hour-and-a-half of sun. The date of our release is not yet set, so we are still waiting. Roberto and Giorgio have already been released, along with the former Dominican, Maurizio. Fernando, Ivo, Tito, and I are still here. Tito is included in the list of prisoners to be exchanged for the Swiss ambassador, but the government is still putting off a final decision. We have suffered a great deal during these fourteen months in prison, but we are well and in good spirits because we know that this is the road we must follow. We have had much support from our brothers in the faith, including Archbishop Paulo Evaristo[57] and the apostolic nuncio. We realize that we are prisoners here so that others may be free, and our hope makes us content.

Pray for us, and rest assured that we are offering our meager suffering to the Lord in the hope that he may grant grace and blessings to your community. An affectionate hug to you all.

90

December 31

Dear Cousin, it was a great joy for me to receive your letter and best wishes on this last day of the year. I am replying immediately primarily because I want to get back in touch with you. I value our friendship.

In your letter you told me that you're trying to integrate your life with the world's, that you have come to realize that "structures depersonalize us." This is a marvelous insight, particularly coming as it does from a city like Rome. We too have been thinking about the same things, and we have reached a conclusion that will not be pleasing to many people: This structure is not undergoing renewal, it is doomed to die. New wine cannot be put into old wineskins, a new patch cannot be sewn on threadbare material. The experiments in renewal that we have seen so far are for the most part artificial. Many people think that renewal means working outside the cloister and earning your own living. This is a necessity of the times. In our desacralized world, the cleric has lost his social function because no one derives vital benefits from cultic worship. At the same time the bourgeoisie no longer supports the church because the church is gradually coming to oppose bourgeois values. So we are obliged to go out and work, but often in jobs that have no apostolic thrust to them. We become enmeshed in the gears of the capitalist system. We "experience life."

But Jesus did not create fishermen-apostles. He took fishermen and made them apostles. We should have the sense to imitate him, to make working priests. For even though we hold jobs, we still live in luxurious houses such as only the rich can afford. So do we really deserve to be called disciples of the poor fishermen of Galilee?

Yes, structures are depersonalizing us, because they have gradually become more important than the gospel. Within these structures we are thought of and treated like helpless children. Naiveté has corroded our critical spirit. We have become masks of blind obedience to the details of our discipline. In our cloisters we are molded into mummies, and creative initiative is condemned as lack of discipline. Alongside our well-appointed houses we have built schools to educate the bourgeoisie, setting our seal of approval on their right to possess *things* in a world where most people possess nothing but hunger and misery. We have lost the apostles' daring. We have given our blessing to European colonialism in Asia, Africa, and Latin America. Time and time again in mission lands we have tried to proclaim the gospel in French and English, and we have drunk deep at the well of social and racial prejudice. To conceal the fact that the skin of the black is repugnant to us, we have said that he is "not very intelligent," that he practices "evil customs," that he is a "savage." We doubt the honesty of the mulatto; we consider Orientals "primitive." But God is not bound by our classifications, as I have discovered here in prison.

I came here filled with lofty intentions. I was going to bring the gospel to these "creatures"—thieves, murderers, brutes you'd be afraid to meet in broad daylight. *But God was here long before I arrived.* Believe me, it is they who have revealed Christ to me. Before we arrived, he was here with them, accomplishing the redemption of the world. They are crucified alongside Jesus. Whose fault is it? Our fault: because we have closed our eyes to human misery, closed our windows against the sight of the slums, avoided the red-light districts, and adopted the bourgeois lifestyle available only to the privileged few.

Living with these people here, I have learned how despicable are our prudence through which we avoid these people, our customs through which we shirk the radicalism of the gospel, our ever-so-sensible counsels through which we convert no one, our lethargy disguised as patience in the face of oppression and social inequality and institutionalized violence.

We have faith in these new stirrings of the Holy Spirit within the church. Perhaps the Spirit has cast us into the world's darkness so that we may learn to view history differently. This suffering is profoundly redemptive.

This is the last evening of the year. As we did at Christmas, the prisoners in each cell along the corridor have formed samba lines. Our sorrows are forgotten and our hopes rekindled. We pray, and we offer up part of this cup of suffering for your sake and your community's. Is Sister Matilde there with you? If she is, give her a big hug for me. Pray for the church in Brazil, for it is living through a difficult time. An affectionate and nostalgic hug for you.

91

To his cousin Maria

December 31

(. . .) There are three Dominicans left in prison with me: Fernando, Ivo, and Tito. Tito is included in the list of prisoners demanded in exchange for the Swiss ambassador, but the negotiations have bogged down. Roberto was freed on October 28 after he had attempted to commit suicide by slitting both wrists. It was the psychological effect of prison life that led him to it. It was not an act of weakness but the protest of a man who had been in prison for almost a year without any charge whatever having been lodged against him. Maurizio, who has left the order (he decided to leave even before his arrest), was freed in November. Our Christmas gift was the release of Giorgio, an Italian, on December 24. There had been no charge against him either. So the four of us are left, waiting for a trial whose date has not yet been set. We are accused of a "crime," namely, that we hid people wanted as subversives by the police and helped them to flee the country. This is an offense according to Brazilian law, but not according to church tradition. Church precedent for aiding fugitives dates from the time when Mary, Joseph, and the child Jesus fled into Egypt to escape Herod's persecution—as I told the Joint Military Council.

There are more than three hundred political prisoners here, both men and women. For seven months there were forty of us in a cell that had room for twenty. For four months I slept on the floor. In September the inmates organized protest demonstrations against the terrible prison conditions and the excessive slowness of the judicial proceedings. Because Giorgio went on a hunger strike, retaliatory measures were directed against us priests. We were taken from prison and sent separately to different barracks. I spent twenty days in solitary confinement in a cell belonging to the cavalry barracks. It measured one meter by three, with hardly room for a bunk. It had no water or sanitary facilities, and I was only allowed to use the washroom once a day—at 8:00 A.M. I faced total solitude there, surrounded by soldiers but unable to exchange a single word with anyone. My only reading material was my New Testament. I was later transferred to headquarters where conditions were slightly better. There at least I could wash up, because there was a water faucet in the cell.

At the end of October we were brought back to Tiradentes prison. We were kept completely separate from the other prisoners, confined in cell 17. It measures two and one-half by six meters. The walls are damp and gray, and there are a lot of holes in the ceiling. So there is a constant dripping of water when it rains. At the back of the cell is a water pipe with·a faucet. There we wash up and get water to drink and to cook with. We cook our own food that is sent to us from the monastery because the prison food is unbearable. We get out of the cell for an hour and a half in the sun only twice a week, and we have visiting hours once every two weeks.

We spend our time in prison reading, doing calisthenics, and studying theology. We are not idle. Every evening we get together for prayer. We recite the Psalms, chant hymns, and receive the body of our Lord. We have not received permission to celebrate Mass, but the chaplain of the military police comes with consecrated hosts every so often.

For me all this represents a revival of the life lived by the church during the first three centuries of its existence. It would be incredible if the church were not present somehow in prisons under a regime that oppresses the human person. Here we are in fellowship with "the wretched of the earth." We are in communion with those who have been invited to the Lord's banquet. All this is grace, as is any suffering endured in a Christian spirit.

I can assure you that prison has effected radical trans-formation—a profound conversion—in us. Behind these bars many things lose the value they once had, and new discoveries turn us into new people. It is good for the church to go through prison. There it rediscovers the way that Christ had pointed out, the way of poverty and persecution. (. . .)

1971

92

January 2

Dearest Mom and Dad, my first letter of the year is to you. I was hoping to send it by T., but I don't think it will be ready in time. She came to see me. Her decision to come to São Paulo seems sound to me. There comes a time when it's important to take off on your own.

We had our New Year's Eve party here in prison. It was pretty much the Christmas party all over again. We sang everything we knew, in a concert that lasted from eleven at night to three in the morning. Very lively and very off-key. I listened more than I sang. I don't have the gift of song, which belongs to the birds and which God has kindly granted to some people. But my three companions sang till they were hoarse. They are the most singular trio that I have ever encountered. Tito knows the lyrics of all the songs, even the old *boleros* that were popular at the same time as the maxi-skirt. Ivo knows the tunes, and Fernando shouts them out. From every cell a small chorus sang together, making the whole prison resonate. And hands thrusting through the bars beat time on the heavy iron doors.

One year has ended, another begun. For some of us it means one year less in prison, for others one year more of waiting.

141

We, for instance, don't know how much longer we will have to stay here. Now rumor has it that we'll be out soon, and we hope the rumor turns out to be true. But rumor does neither us nor you any good. It's better to assume that we'll get out when the discharge papers arrive. These flights of fancy may nurture hope, but the prison bars remain impassable as ever, with us on the inside. I prefer not to cherish any illusions because nothing is more dangerous for a prisoner than impatience. Imprisonment is not like illness, in which the doctor's contagious optimism is a real psychological aid to the patient's recovering. This is different, as I noticed with Giorgio. In the last six months of his internment somebody came by at least once a week to assure him that he would be released the following week. Result: As the weeks passed and his irritability mounted, he gradually lost all power of concentration. So it is better to wait for freedom to come to you than to try to grab it. I suspect that the family's impatience is greater than mine.

(. . .) And I see people here who will not go free for ten or twenty years. There was a kid here, just recently transferred to a penitentiary, twenty-nine years old and sentenced to sixty-seven years in prison. He has already served ten. I have thought about it for a long time, and I ask myself how in the name of justice it can take sixty-seven years in prison to rehabilitate a nineteen-year-old! Compared to people like him, I have no right to feel sorry for myself, particularly since I always knew what I was getting into and why. Some people are convicted for actions for which they are not wholly responsible. In a sudden burst of anger they commit an act that has irreparable consequences. There are prisoners who will have to pay for such a lapse with many years of their lives. For example, I think I would not be able [censored]. A longing bearhug to you all.

93

To the Dominican community in São Paulo

January 12

Dear Friends, it is not too late to thank you for your best wishes. The past few days I've been very busy with my Christmas mail because I always answer everyone who writes to me. Besides the mail from our families we get letters offering to pray for us from many Catholic convents. It does us good. Personally I have blind faith in the value of prayer although I don't care to turn it into a list of petitions. In God's plan nothing happens by chance. So I know that I will get out of here at the right moment, no sooner and no later, though everybody (including me) hopes that the right moment won't be too long in coming.

In prison it is important to wait patiently for the moment of liberation. You have to know how to derive benefit from every aspect of this experience. The fact is we are learning a great deal about people and about life. Particularly now, because we are in a cell-block of common prisoners, despite the fact that by law we are entitled to a special prison of our own. Here we see the other side of the coin. Being in this prison puts us in contact with all those who are detested and condemned by our society, and there is no doubt that it alters our personalities. Our web of illusions is torn apart by every breeze that blows. It becomes plain to see that we do not live in the best of all possible worlds.

Though I have been in prison for fourteen months, I can't say that I've gotten used to it. Even birds don't get used to it, much less people. But intelligence enables us to adapt to even the most deplorable circumstances; at least it keeps us from being overwhelmed by them. In a time of suffering we must preserve our dignity and recognize the fact that this trial is not in vain. It is only one moment in our chapter of history, which keeps moving ahead. I have every confidence in the future.

Now there are three of us Dominicans here. We are in a small cell with gray and white walls and a triple-barred window. At this time of year the heat is almost unbearable, but we still manage to read, do some handicrafts, exercise a bit. It is not exactly a debilitating routine. In a prison filled with inmates something new is always happening, particularly right now when there is a lot of coming and going.

I hope you all are well and I send you a big hug filled with fond memories.

94

To his brothers and sisters

January 14

Dear Ones, everything is OK here. Tito was released Monday morning. For many days he was under extreme tension. He was taken away several times for identification purposes, and he was photographed in the nude. Then he videotaped a statement of his reasons for leaving the country. He stated that his only interest was in saving the ambassador's life. I think he'll have lots of opportunities for study abroad. Probably he'll go to Europe.

So now there are three of us in the cell. We have more room and a situation more conducive to work and study. (. . .)

95

To Pedro

January 20

Dear Pedro, you are quite right in saying that we can't read the Bible without reference to our own condition (being careful not to define our "condition" solely and narrowly as the circumstances of our own life). Through my condition I come to recognize myself in God's word. It's a shame that the church's preaching has not always respected these human conditions, which are simultaneously subjective and objective. Herein lies the mistake of those who concentrate exclusively on the *letter* of the Scripture, a way of thinking that comes of concentrating on the letter of the law. We need only recall the missionary enterprise in colonial Brazil, when the Indians were forced to undergo baptism. Today the pope's frequent appeals for peace are unrelated to objective conditions. People want peace, undoubtedly, but insofar as it is the fruit of justice.

In the notes you sent me I read the following: "The Bible does not purport to transmit a specific cultural and historical view of the world, *because the word of God is adaptable to all.* It seeks to bring all human beings in the course of their lives into contact with Jesus Christ under conditions that make possible a true conversion, both individual and collective. It's this latter aspect of conversion that calls for the transformation of the world in which we live" (p. 7).

There is no denying what you say about the results of conversion (which means fulfillment of the promise through the manifestation of God's kingdom). But I doubt that the word of God is adaptable to *every* cultural and historical view of the world. I think that some views are the negation of God's word: for example, the mechanistic and the liberal views. The first reduces the autonomy of human activity and hence human freedom. The second is fundamentally individualistic and anarchic. Unfortunately the word of the church often adapts itself to this liberal vision, thus flagrantly contradicting the word of God. Many Christians have a subjective and alienated vision of the world that causes them to read the Bible myopically. They cannot break out of the shell that imprisons and corrupts their understanding. If our present is to be explained solely by the past, and its meaning for the future is shown us by the past, then clearly we must consider the Bible to be God's word to us here and now. In other words what God does has continuity in history. It is a permanent and lasting activity. We can perceive it at times, but we can never know all its principles and its instruments. We know that God's activity does not and has not ever reduced the force of human activity. Believe it or not, man tends naturally to act in

145

conformity with God. On the other hand, God's activity intends the good of the world and its people. It does not have as its object single individuals, and it certainly does not propose the triumph of a heavenly kingdom and the dwindling into insignificance of this earthly one. It exists in the world and in time and identifies itself with every longing for justice, progress, freedom, peace, and love. It escapes the limitations of our condition and it does not necessarily well up among those of God's people who constitute the church. It is the activity of the just person for his people. The Bible is precisely the mirror in which this activity is reflected most clearly. So it is clear that God's activity is not present where a concern for the future is lacking, where the present is turned into an absolute and the past into the subject of an incurable nostalgia.

In your notes you say: "The same God who gave direction to our lives in the past continues to do so today. In our present God draws the course of the past toward the future."

This indicates the historical awareness inherent in the Bible and the need to have such awareness in order to understand God's word today. It seems to me that the catechesis based on "salvation history" has not produced such understanding. There are many ways of thinking about history. Many catechists are capable of thinking about it only episodically or allegorically. They know the history of the Hebrew nation as they know the history of the Persian Empire or the French Revolution. They cannot see the present historical moment as part and parcel of salvation history. They do not recognize today as history in process, hence they cannot establish continuity between past and present in salvation history. But if the God of Christians were not present in the currents of today's history, then he would not be the God of Jesus Christ.

So contact with the Bible should make us feel inextricably linked to the past and inescapably committed to the future. But the future will not be brought about by intentions alone, much less by the preservation or perfecting of an inhuman social order. Building the future means breaking with the present because a bad tree cannot bear good fruit. That is what the

Bible teaches us. The Hebrews separated by violence from the Egyptians. They realized that their future called for a new reality, and since they could not persuade the pharaoh, they had to break with him.

Now I ask myself: To what sort of future is the church committed? Can the peace so much desired by everyone come from the hands of those who provoke war? Can the future arise from the ruins of a social order that has reduced the person to the level of a tool of production? The difficulty experienced by the church in answering such questions indicates how much we lack historical awareness that would immerse us in fashioning the future, that is not limited to vague and abstract yearnings but committed concretely and specifically to the struggle for such a future.

Like the prophets, people who plunge headlong into denunciations of the present in order to inspire commitment to the future risk their necks. So, like our bishops, people prefer simply to decry the "abuses" of the present and to believe that the future will arise spontaneously out of a corrupt and agonizing present. The minority of activists who choose to break with the present must face up to the painful consequences of their choice. Living for the future, they can expect only cruel persecution in the present. It is the age-old dialectic of history.

Perhaps, to get on with the subject, we should define more carefully what we mean by history. From the Bible we can deduce a theological concept. But I get the impression that Christians are not yet capable of interest in this theological concept, much less in any other concept of a philosophical nature. They accept history only with subtitles—a chronicle of Past Events involving Great Men. There are people who think they know the history of the Roman Empire because they know a bit about emperors and their conquests. That is like trying to recount the history of Brazil through the biographies of its presidents. My first impression is that the church, or rather its teachings, has an idealistic concept of history, one in which events are considered to be independent of human activity, as if history were the motive force of human

147

beings instead of the other way around. This is virtually to "identify history with God." Church teaching also tends to the belief that history is always made by "others," and our task is solely to advise and inspire, to certify and judge. But those who commit themselves to action, who struggle and suffer and endure the pangs of childbirth, will be the "others."

The Bible presents the past as a normative standard. What was the attitude of the people of Israel toward history? They placed themselves in the vanguard of history, consciously fighting for their own liberation and their own future. They admitted their own mistakes and trusted in God's promise. But what is the attitude of contemporary Christians toward history?

Your list of suggestions (p. 32) on learning to read the Bible is very good. The fourth says: "The Bible calls upon us today to recognize that God is journeying with us." We must be imbued with this awareness. God is present in the history that is unfolding around us, that is reported in the newspapers and on TV. But how are we to recognize his presence? It is easy to say that God is present in history. But it is hard to assert God is present in the Vietnam war, in the Middle East, in the struggles of the Black Panthers in the United States and the Jews in the Soviet Union, in the guerrilla movements of Latin America. And yet that is precisely what the Bible teaches us. Cyrus did not have to be virtuous for Isaiah to see him as one sent by the Lord. The important thing was the historical function that Cyrus embodied for Israel at that moment. Hence I can say to you that I can recognize the presence of God in all the wars and revolutions going on today. But why is it that we today cannot glimpse the signs of this presence? The truth is that we are living in contradiction to our own principles. Either the word of God gives us our bearings amid concrete, tangible facts, or it makes no sense to us. We are imprisoned in vague theoretical principles that we don't know how or when to apply. In the West we defend with tooth and nail the individual's right to private property, but in the East we allow the United States to trample on the collective right of a people to be sovereign in its own land.

You write: "The Bible is a book born from people and meant to guide them along their way." It is God's plan for human history. A great responsibility rests on those who are cognizant of this plan by virtue of their faith. Great blame attaches to those who try to shirk their part in carrying out this plan. You are perfectly right when you say, "Today there is no absolute division between textual interpretation and life." But it will not be easy to establish the connection between the two. The long period during which the Bible was a closed book for Catholics is costing us dearly today. It is still not easy to find a Catholic who reads the New Testament, . . . and if you do find one, you don't know if he has managed to take off the blinders that keep him from seeing the light. . . .

I also want to touch upon your fine explanation (pp. 61ff.) of "how the Bible deals with God's activity outside his people." This activity is great, and as divine pedagogy it forces God's people to recognize their mistakes and get back on the right road. The Catholic church has begun to do this with Vatican II. I have no doubt that God is challenging us by inspiring an avowedly atheistic movement that seeks at least to eradicate material misery [censored].

I like your proposal to extend the concept of salvation history to our own history. But we must keep in mind the fact that many people are not capable of discerning in their own history the signs that point to the promised future. There is so much alienation around. We won't break out of stagnation until we break the hold of alienation on our awareness. And this is an extremely difficult thing to do.

Your notes have been extremely enlightening. I forbid you to stop sending me such food for thought. Remember me in your prayers. (. . .)

149

96

To Sister Marike

January 24

Dear Sister, I know that you have been operated on and are now, thank God, convalescing. I'm afraid that at times like these we don't always have the courage to treat suffering as something temporary and bearable. But it should not be difficult for us Christians because we know that the way to Resurrection is through the Cross. That does not mean we should simply resign ourselves. If pain is the result of evil, I don't see why God would want only resignation from us. Instead God asks us to have the courage to face suffering and surmount it. In any case pain does liberate us; this is the discovery we all must make through our own passion.

Today I am more than ever convinced that I cannot complain of my situation; but neither can I call it the will of God. First of all I realize that my suffering is insignificant compared with that of countless other people. I think of whole families living in poverty and hunger, of people born physically or mentally defective, of the common prisoners now in my cell who will tomorrow be taken to police headquarters. . . . Second I think that God would be denying his own goodness if he wished to see us suffer. God wishes us good, peace, joy, well-being, and mutual respect. If I am a prisoner here, it's not God's will but the will of people who judge me to be a political criminal, a danger to the security of the state.

If you are sick, it is a bodily disorder that science is trying to overcome. Nevertheless it is certain that God intervenes in every moment and in each event of our lives. It is not God's will that I find myself here, but his will is revealed to me in this place just as I am sure it is being revealed to you. He asks us to be strong, to be wise enough to carry our cross and not succumb, because his yoke is sweet and his burden light. He also asks us to transform our suffering into an act of solidarity with all those who suffer in the world. This is the communion of saints, which leads us to liberation, restores our strength, and fills us with courage.

So we need fear nothing. We don't let pain grind us down and triumph over us. Only for the Christian can suffering be a freely chosen option, as it was for Jesus Christ. He chose the way of the cross, not out of masochism but because every true redemption, like every new life, is born of pain.

People are talking about the canonization of a Polish priest who was pastor of a village during World War II. When the Nazis invaded Poland, they decreed that ten civilians would be summarily shot for every German soldier killed. A soldier was killed, whereupon the Nazis rounded up all the men of this village and took them to the town square. Among them, unbeknownst to the Germans, was the priest. Ten villagers were picked at random to be shot for the death of the soldier. The priest was not one of them, but a workingman standing near him, father of five small children, was. Immediately the priest stepped forward and asked to die in his place. Since the selection had been random, the exchange was permitted; the children's father was spared, and the priest was taken away. The Nazis quickly discovered that he was a priest. The other nine they shot; him they locked up alone without food or water. Days later, he died, overcome by the torture of total abandonment.

Can we say that this priest willed his suffering? No. He willed to save the life of a man who had five children to take care of. We should not will that our suffering be extinguished but that while it exists it should bear fruit in Christ's mystical body for the liberation and salvation of humanity. (. . .)

97

To a friend

January 31

Dearest Alice, prison does not afford much happiness, it is true, but it does lead us to many discoveries. I can say that 1970 was as important a year for me as 1965, the year of my novitiate. In 1965 I learned the nature of faith; now I know how to live it. I may not be able to carry what I've learned much further, but I'm sure that I can never again know the tranquil conscience of the Christian who goes to Mass on Sunday and is content with a minimum of spirituality.

In prison you realize that it's impossible to be free simply by chance and furthermore that we are prisoners of the many useless limitations we allow life to impose on us. At least here the complete physical limitation—living behind bars for an indefinite length of time—completely dissolves all the other limitations that we have acquired from a bourgeois education full of falsity. You cannot cheat here. It's a clean game, and the only thing that counts is the truth of each individual. Words, appearances, and illusions lose their significance. We are all reduced to our human essence. You see yourself in a mirror, stripped of disguises and fantasies. Two alternatives are open to you: You can take flight in laziness, fear, or madness; or you can break with the past and commit yourself to the future, though it cost you your life.

After a certain length of time (more psychological than chronological), the prisoner begins to glimpse the moment of liberation. It is like a hoped-for vision of resurrection. Freedom does not mean simply physical liberty. It also entails a new manner of living, a new set of values, the overcoming of old habits. For us Christians it means continuing in the poverty that we have come to know here. It means a new spirit of service, one that is much simpler, more radical, and coherent.

That's why this past year has been so important for me. I have come to half a dozen conclusions that I consider fundamental to my life. No one can remain the same after spending so much time in the darkness of this world. For lack of light we have learned to see ourselves in the dark. We have learned to see into things, to perceive the essential qualities by which they exist and are defined and expressed. We realize now that our task is a terrible one. If we have faith besides, then nothing can go on as before. All that remains for us is to figure out how to act from here.

In short I have no reason to complain. Despite everything, so profound an experience is worth the cost. I know that on my own I would never have encountered certain situations that prison forces upon me. Finding myself here, I accept these situations and try to make the most of them. (. . .)

98

January 31

Dear Ernesto, (. . .) For two days we have not had a drop of water in this cell, which seems like a pressure-cooker. The roof of this cell block is not tiled, so the ceiling gets scorching hot during the day. And there is no ventilation. Don't try to imagine what it's like; it's indescribable. It feels as if there will be a riot at any moment. In the overcrowded cells the smell is unbearable. When it rains, we try to collect a little water through the holes in the roof. But the heat is intolerable. Prisoners shout for water day and night, but our cries echo uselessly down the dismal prison corridors. At these times we see how easily a human being can cease to be rational and become a brute. Every so often we get a pitcher of dirty water from God knows where; we boil it before drinking. With every sip we take, our bourgeois habits—already pretty well corroded by these fourteen months in prison—crumble a bit more. Even our scale of values has been altered by our circumstances here. Many things lose their importance to us, and new criteria appear. In other words we undergo a change in social class. Our whole worldview is profoundly changed —from theory to practice. Whoever doesn't adapt gives way to despair.

Throughout this period my chief concern has been the church of God in Brazil. Only now do I see clearly my vocation within it. We have a great task to carry out. We must stop pointing to the past with the Gospels in our hands. We must live and learn how to live. I am trying to analyze, as scientifically as possible and without confining myself wholly to the realm of ideas, the impediments to and possibilities of living a

Christian life. It would take too long to discuss it now, but I can assure you that this preoccupation makes time fly for me in prison. How do we overcome the dualism between faith and life? Between divine revelation and history? Between faith and politics? I make every attempt to put this period of seclusion to good use. It is cruel, but it is not in vain. Many things will be born in this darkness.

Your being in court when I gave my deposition made me so happy. Christ was right: We shouldn't be concerned about what to say; the important thing is to bear witness.

Thanks for your prayers. I pray for you too.

99

To Pedro

February 2

Dear Pedro, your postcard made us very happy. It had a particularly good effect on the psychological atmosphere here. Locked up all day in this pressure-cooker and melting in this terrible summer heat, it was a real relief to look at the snow-covered mountains of Albiez-le-Vieux and to know that you had thought of us there. Here we would be satisfied with a sliver of ice to melt in the warm water that flows from our tap after boiling its way through the city pipes. The ceiling of our cell is red hot.

I was once up at an altitude of 5300 meters. There was no snow, only ice. I didn't have oxygen, or even adequate clothing. Being inexperienced, I started drinking whisky. My heart began to beat so hard I thought it was going to jump out of my mouth. I came down the Andean slopes in a jolting old pull-man car and was immediately taken to an oxygen tank.

Today I'm having the opposite experience. Here we have oxygen but no ventilation. Our cell has two iron bars and a plate of sheet metal with minuscule holes in it. The door is a slab of dark iron with the usual barred opening in the middle. The oxygen is inside us; it is the force that enables us to rise above this oppressive situation and face it courageously. Many people who come up to visit us wonder whether they could stand prison. The fact is that there are cases of deep depression and even of madness.

At dawn this prison is the image of hell. Banging and shouting and songs of desperation reverberate through the cell block, exploding from hearts steeped in bitterness. These outbursts are typical of the common prisoners with whom we are thrown together. Political prisoners have more endurance, particularly more solidarity. None of us is alone. The important thing is to succeed in conquering our old habits. By now we are no longer upset at living together in a cell where the sanitary facilities are in the middle of the room near our beds and where there is only one faucet. You lose your physical freedom but you gain the freedom of awareness. You learn to accept the radicalization of your life.

At the age of twenty-six I suddenly realize that all my adolescent dreams have gone up in smoke. I feel very young and very realistic about the future! Faith is too serious a thing not to effect profound transformations in us. But you cannot foresee this. Equally unforeseeable is everything that brings us fulfillment (love, for example) and everything that leads us to the truth of ourselves—such things as poverty, prison, pain, struggle, and hope in a future that will flower in our hands though today we clutch only a thorny stalk. All the principles that once resounded in my head and made me the prototype of the Western Christian have now broken to smithereens. (. . .)

I can never manage to leave out my prison experience when I write. It is an exceptional period, and I cannot let it go by without making the most of it. Your family is in our prayers. An affectionate hug for you.

100

February 7

Dear Little Cousins (please don't call me uncle, or else I'll feel old. . . . Just between ourselves, we are brothers, but keep it quiet, otherwise your mom might also feel old. . .).

Today I'm going to tell you a story, not a bedtime story, but a waking-up story. . . .

Once upon a time there was a man who could never resign himself to the fact that he was not like a bird. He felt imprisoned because he couldn't warble and fly and be free like a bird. No matter how hard he tried, he could never manage to get off the ground. He felt nailed to the ground because he couldn't fly like the birds, who live in the vast expanses of space and time. He would open his mouth to speak, and out would come only grunts that no one understood. He would never be able to sing like the birds, with that beautiful sweetness.

One day this man decided that the best thing to do was to reverse the nature of his unsatisfied desire. And he had the *power* to do it. Since he couldn't be like the birds, he would try to become their master.

The man built a trap, put a worm inside, and set the trap on the branch of a tree. A lively bird, flying around the tree, noticed the worm and swooped down to take this food for his children. The man was close by watching. No sooner did the bird's foot touch the edge of the trap than it sprang shut and the bird was caught. The bird beat his wings furiously to escape the snare, but to no avail. His leg remained caught. The man observed his desperation without pity; indeed he took delight in the bird's anguish. The bird would fly no more, its children would die of hunger, and its song would grow sad as the winter nights. The man approached the trap and grabbed the bird. He was going to strangle it to death, but then he realized that the bird's suffering would end too quickly if he did that. It would be better to shut the bird in a cage where he could hear him cry for his lost liberty.

The bird was imprisoned in a cage. No more flights over fields and gardens, no more scent of leaves and flowers in bloom. The man took delight in seeing the bird a prisoner like himself. There was only one hitch: The bird could still sing, and he could not.

As time went on, the man added many more traps and invented new snares to catch birds. He replaced the old cage with a huge birdhouse in which he kept all his prisoners. *It gave him pleasure to look upon his imprisoned birds because they testified to his power.* Somehow it made him feel more free even though he could never be a bird.

Birds, however, reproduce faster than people. Although the man could imprison some birds, the rest remained beautiful and free as the man could never be. Faced with whole flocks singing anthems of freedom in the sky, the man was forced to admit his powerlessness. But he persevered in his wickedness and continued capturing birds when he could.

When his time came, the man died. From his grave a tree grew, spreading its leafy branches high in the air. One glorious summer afternoon a huge flock of birds descended and began to build their nests.

My dear little cousins, I love you very much, and I think of you often and I miss you. Some day we will all be together again. Then we will be able to sing and to fly like the birds. . . .

A great big hug.

101

To his parents

February 18

(. . .) This morning we had a visit from the apostolic nuncio. He came with Bishop Benedito Ulhoa, the chaplain of the Pontifical Catholic University, and Father Angelo Giannola, the episcopal vicar for the southern district of São Paulo. Our newest fellow prisoner, Father Giulio Vicini, comes from there. As usual, the nuncio brought us a touch of happiness and some cigarettes. He said he had been to see you at home and that he will come to dinner again as soon as I've been freed. He was impressed with Mom's tranquillity, and said that "any other mother would be in tears." He didn't say anything about the annual meeting of the National Episcopal Conference except that you two were there. We are waiting to hear about it from you. (. . .)

Right now I'm reading about the results of the bishops' meeting in Belo Horizonte.[59] I gather from the newspapers that for the first time a bishop has gone on record as demanding an inquiry and has been backed up by the rest of the episcopate. Times have changed. It appears that the era of the silent church—the church that couldn't take a stand when we were arrested—is over. Now I understand Jesus' words to the authorities who wanted him to silence the acclaim of the crowds: "If they were to keep silent, the very stones would cry out."

It's best to have faith in the Holy Spirit. The election of the new board of directors seems to me a good thing. The cardinals' primacy is at an end. The board has ceased to be a rubber-stamp for authority and has begun to exercise its executive function. I think that the seventies will be a time of decision for the Brazilian church. I get the impression that we are beginning to reap the first fruits of the seeds sown by Catholic Action in the sixties. But these fruits are still tender, delicate, and weak, borne on a tree that sways in every breeze.

The letter to Bishop Valdir was also a success. I can well imagine the joy it must have given him. (. . .) I am thinking of him, now a frail old bishop in the Northeast who has walked on water without any public support from those around him. He has been slandered and silenced, judged by some and condemned by others. No one has spoken out and said that he is on the side of the gospel. I think the church of the future will venerate him as a saint and a prophet. (. . .)

On the other hand, I was frankly not pleased with the letter they sent Father Domingos. It should have been more incisive. It opens: "The central commission has received your letter requesting a statement from the episcopate concerning the brothers who are prisoners in São Paulo." Does that mean that if Father Domingos had not written the letter, no one would have spoken out? The whole first paragraph is useless. The letter goes on to say that "the imprisonment and trial has dragged on for fifteen months." But it is stated impersonally, as if they were afraid to mention the prisoners by name. The letter is good where it notes that our plight is the same as that of many prisoners, but it does not publish (on purpose?) the bishops' opinion of our case. The pope has already shown his sympathy and sent us his blessing. The papal secretary of state has said that there is no evidence against us. Our order has given us its full support. Yet the bishops are unable to say whether we are innocent or guilty. They are waiting for the verdict of the Justice Department of the military regime. There is a kind of implied support in the fact that while they say nothing in our favor, they say nothing against us either. *In dubio pro reo.* [60] Isolated voices don't count. (. . .)

102

To Sister Ruth

February 27

Dear Cousin, your letter comes to us like a friendly and encouraging presence. It's the kind of support that comforts us most. It makes us feel that we are not alone, that we no longer live in a silent church. The church's silence, unfortunately, was what first impressed us after our arrest. After so much talk about the Christian presence in today's world, some priests were astonished and dumbfounded by our praxis. It reminded me of Jesus' conversation with his disciples when he revealed that everything foretold earlier he would have to live in his own body: "From that time Jesus began to make it clear to his disciples that he had to go to Jerusalem, and there to suffer much from the elders, chief priests, and doctors of the law; to be put to death and to be raised again on the third day.

159

At this Peter took him by the arm and began to rebuke him: 'Heaven forbid!' he said. 'No, Lord, this shall never happen to you' " (Matt. 15:21–23).

Peter had no trouble assenting to ideas and programs, but he could not accept such things happening *in reality*. He was afraid to face reality. He thought that the gospel pertained *to others*, to the church, but not to his particular community of disciples and apostles. Peter wanted a Christ for himself, a nicely protected Christ, safely removed from life's contradictions and conflicts, from cruel suffering, and from the cross. He didn't want a Christ who would follow his commitment to its final consequences. Prudent Peter thought he knew and could interpret God's thoughts. What was Jesus thinking of! How could he die on a cross like a common criminal! Such fates were for *other people*, not for Christ and his disciples.

Today, echoing Peter's logic, we may ask: What are you thinking of! A church of the oppressed, the ragged, the starving, the alienated, the persecuted and imprisoned? An outlaw church?! Jesus, however, did not have the patience to explain to Peter why he was mistaken; nor did he keep silent in the hope that Peter would understand him later. Jesus got angry because Peter hadn't grasped the essence of the mystery of redemption. He must have thought: "Is all I've taught only a subject for sermons rather than a rule for living? What you want is a community of 'Establishment' Christians, well dressed and on friendly terms with the rich and powerful, supporters of the status quo. No risk, no daring, no radical break with the way things are." So angry was Jesus that he saw his friend as the very incarnation of the Enemy: "Away with you, Satan; you are a stumbling block to me. You think as men think, not as God thinks" (Matt. 16:23). The fact is that human beings do want a church triumphant rather than suffering, a church upheld by the laws rather than one in hiding in the catacombs, a church capable of pardoning sin rather than one capable of extirpating evil at its root.

This is the experience of God of which you speak in your letter. It's the experience of walking the same road that he walked, of learning through faith about things that are beyond

160

poor human reasoning. Prison enables us to live this experience of God intensely. There are five of us in this cell now—Fernando, Ivo, and I are Dominicans; Father Giulio Vicini[61] and Laercio Barros, a seminarian from the diocese of Lins, are with us. Laercio is serving a one-year term, which will end in 1972, for using a book by Michel Quoist (*The Diary of Anna Maria*). Father Vicini will be interrogated by a military court next Monday. We Dominicans were interrogated last October, almost a year after our arrest, and as yet the date of our sentencing has not been fixed. We are serving the sentence ahead of time.

Recently we have been visited regularly by the new archbishop of São Paulo.[62] Last week the apostolic nuncio, Bishop Mozzoni, came to see us, bringing us as usual gladness and cigarettes. We are expecting a visit from our superior general[63] in April.

We thank your community for their prayers that our suffering may bear fruit within the church and that our spirits may be stronger than the bars that confine us. With you we wait for the Lord's Easter.

103

To his family

March 3

Dearest Parents and Brothers and Sisters, last Sunday Father Ettore Torrini, who has spent twenty-one years in Acre,[64] came to celebrate Mass in our cell. (. . .) The mass was simple—as life in prison and the things that pertain to God are simple. There is more intensity in the Masses here than I have ever found in Masses celebrated on the outside. Christ is more intimately, almost tangibly, present. They remind me of the catacombs. Father Torrini wept because something here reminded him of certain experiences of his in the East that evidently made a profound impression on his life. How much more beautiful Mass is when the chalice is a cup, the altar a wooden bench, the church a small cell, and the worshippers are prisoners. Over the centuries we have made things too complicated. We have transformed the familiar, unstudied rite into pomp and ceremony, the dialogue into protocol. Now we have reached the critical point. We don't cast off ceremony because we don't want to offend other people's sensibilities, and we wait for these sensibilities to change so that we can cast off ceremony.

People have sent us a huge stack of Italian, French, and German magazines (in the German ones I can only look at the pictures). In the *Paris Match* of October 1969 were several letters written at various times by John XXIII to his family. They are taken from an anthology of his letters that is about to be published. Here is an excerpt from one of the letters:

> I cannot in conscience, as a Christian and a priest, vote for the Fascists. Everyone is free to judge the matter from his own point of view. In the end we will find out who was right. Do what you think is best. In my own opinion, however, you would do better to vote for the popular slate if you have the freedom to vote as you choose. If that freedom does not exist, then it might be better to stay at home and let things take their course. Otherwise you could be in for trouble. I am sure of one thing: Italy's salvation cannot come from Mussolini, even though he may be an able man. The goals he envisions might be good ones, but the means he employs are wrong and contrary to the gospel. . . . Affectionately, your Don Angelo.

He wrote that in April 1924. What historical insight that man had! (. . .)

104

To a Dominican fellow student

March 6

Dear Robert, locked up in this cell, listening to the rain beating down on the grating, I keep reading your letter over and over again. It gives me comfort, peace, and courage. I feel now that suffering is worthwhile, that every sorrow is a harbinger of redemption. Although I would not exactly have chosen this, I know that God has chosen precisely this for me.

As you put it in your letter, "I am simply carried along by Him." Sometimes I resist, but the power of attraction that he exerts on me is stronger still. I think he asks a great deal of me, more than I have strength or ability to give. Who am I, Lord? In my inmost heart, I swear, I envy the humble lay brother in a Trappist monastery, who gives glory to God in the silence of his anonymous life, milking cows and making cheese. But then reason prevails. Once I have put my hand to the plow, I have no right to turn back (Luke 9:62). I know that salvation lies there where the cross looms, roughhewn and terrible. If death should overtake me now, I could die knowing that, despite all my mistakes, I have tried to live the teaching of Jesus.

You ask me to write something relevant to your calling that would be "less of reason and theology and more of inner experience." I'll tell you what I feel—which doesn't mean that I live accordingly. I have still more breaking with the past to do before I'll be able to say that it is now Christ who lives in me (Gal. 2:20).

What really does exist in me is an irresistible attraction to God. Whether they know it or not, people speak of this attraction using many names, such as justice, peace, progress, or freedom, and they live it out on the political, economic, religious, or social plane. For me this divine summons is made explicit in Jesus Christ, and it is handed down and brought to life in the community of faith that is the church. This is the origin of what I feel: a profound and all-encompassing love for the church of Jesus Christ. It is the church that has made him known to me. It is the church in which his word lives, errors and omissions notwithstanding. Indeed it is these defects that make it ever clearer to me that the church is a human community and not a divine one, a historical community and not a heavenly one. The church is us poor sinners continually seeking to become one with him. If what I am doing is meaningless for the church, then I have not achieved what I was really looking for. I have given my life to the church. Today in all humility I realize this is true. Not a week has gone by since I was a child that I have not been occupied with meetings or readings or some activity for the spread of the gospel and the growth of the church. So I love this fulcrum of my life, this mainspring of my existence. It pains me when the church is unfaithful to Jesus' word. It pains me that we are not like the poor fishermen of Galilee. It pains me when I find myself un-Christian. And I become very jealous when anyone tries to take over the church and use it like a prostitute.

The church's mission is gratuitous service to human beings. We cannot delude ourselves that we are serving the church if we do not serve people, particularly the neediest. When I took my vows, I realized that they set the seal on my commitment to serve others. A promise to give myself to the service of others would therefore have made more sense than the vows I took.

Thanks to the secular upbringing and training that you and I have had, we have never found it possible to separate the church and the world. There is no such dualism in our thinking or our lives and this makes certain things a lot easier. It saves us from thinking of service to the church and service to the world as mutually exclusive commitments. The church is a movement in the world. Its mission arises there and is carried out there. This perspective reveals most clearly the existential aspects of contemporary vows within the traditional institutions of religious life in the church.

Let me say a little first about how I think we should live these vows and then about how I look on them as a whole in relation to the meaning of contemporary religious life. When we talk about the vows of obedience, chastity, and poverty, we could be talking about vows of fidelity, gratuitous generosity, and justice. What's important is that the three really are one and that they represent a choice. Unfortunately, in this matter we are still subject to ecclesiastical jurisdiction. But since this is the *form* through which we make official our commitment to the religious life, we see that these vows can indeed be made meaningful.

I think that obedience is owed to God, who speaks to us through the Bible, the church, the world, and history. God speaks through the signs of the times. If my superior or my community are at variance with the will of God as I perceive it in real life, then I owe them no obedience. I owe obedience to the poor whom Jesus served. I owe obedience to the pathways of hope in the life of my time, to concrete and effective love for others. I do not owe obedience to anything that renders me less free, less human, less committed, less aware. I do not owe obedience to laws that shackle human beings and stifle the spread of the gospel; to traditions that drain Christian life of its pristine force; to anything that makes me look more obedient and less Christian, more prudent and less evangelical. Obedience cannot mean cowardice, conformism, egotism, overprotectedness, and fear of risk. Obedience should lead me to the cross, not to the throne (see Matt. 16:21–23).

When Jesus revealed to Peter that the road he must take was the road to the cross, Peter objected. He wanted a community without problems. He wanted Jesus to walk in his footsteps rather than the other way around. Peter wanted to preserve the appearances of respectability, to prevent Jesus from dying like an outlaw and tarnishing the community's image. In *The Brothers Karamazov* the Grand Inquisitor will say the same thing to the outlaw in whom he recognizes Christ. Jesus did not restrain his anger at Peter's way of thinking; he saw in his friend the image of his enemy. And what about us? How many times have we, in the name of obedience, sinned by omission? How many times have we failed to see that God's ways seem foolish to people? How many times are we more heedful of the letter of the law than the appeals of the living?

As far as the vow of chastity is concerned, you know what I think. It is to free us for service to others, but it is also a great renunciation. It is a charism if God permits us to live so without its withering our emotions. From one moment to the next I can expect to feel the need for a female companion. Life itself, the greatest gift we have received, is the fruit of human love. It is wonderful that I feel the attraction of this love and that faith enables me to live it in a new dimension. I am deliberately and firmly set on making this renunciation, but the resultant void not even God can fill, for that would amount to altering human nature itself. Love remains, and it is beautiful to experience the capacity to love outside the confines of the flesh. Those who limit themselves to these confines have not yet reached the starting point of love. There is no fulfillment in love unless that love is generous and expansive. A couple who think they love each other but don't love other human beings have not yet discovered love. A man's love for other people is mediated through his love for his wife, and vice versa. This love is most completely expressed in the physical union of the two, which is the sign of their communion with other human beings. God's gift of faith permits a mystical expression of this same union. This is no abstraction. The love I feel for people becomes more real insofar as I freely place myself at their service.

On a more personal plane it is obvious that I love some people, to whom I am bound by ties of friendship and fellowship, more than others. Christ himself had preferences, and this is a mystery that only the gratuitous nature of love can explain. If these ties were to be established with a woman, then I would naturally discover all her beauty and be enchanted by her charms. But I know the boundary between gift and possession. If I don't include having a family among my plans for the future, then I have no reason to encourage a state of affairs requiring exclusive possession, particularly since I see no relation between love and any kind of sentimental escapade. It is people damaged by egotism who get involved in sentimental adventures which are always an attempt to be loved.

So celibacy has meaning if faith enables us to express mutual reciprocal human love through the exclusive mediation of God, if celibacy itself permits us to recognize how great and real human love is, above and beyond mere physical union. After all, physical union itself is never a point of departure, as the pervasive bourgeois culture makes people think. It is rather a final goal of full mystical and physical communion. This communion is a harbinger of our mystical union with God that is made possible by contemplative action. But mystical union with God is not a privilege reserved for the celibate. Purity, daring, and detachment are not inaccessible to a married person. Indeed Jesus chose married men to be his apostles, and I have known many married men capable of a selflessness that few religious can equal. . . .

So I cannot evaluate celibacy in terms of advantages or disadvantages. Marriage does not diminish people, and celibacy does not exalt them. *Celibacy is a gift. One accepts a gift from God not as a privilege but as a responsibility undertaken for the sake of a mission.* I accept this gift in complete consciousness of my masculinity. It is important not to confuse celibacy with sexlessness. No one loses his sex because he is celibate, and it disturbs me that many religious should give that very impression.

I don't want to pursue this discussion any further, however, because I would end up going beyond the realm of personal experience and reality. I thank God for the gift he has granted me, and I hope my ability to love will continually increase.

As for poverty, I am embarrassed to talk about it. First of all, because I am not poor. I was educated in middle-class comfort, and I have lived my life under the spell of its alienating attractions. I have not struggled to survive; I have not been dehumanized by the production system. At the same time, however, I have never had income or human relationships that were supported by this form of alienation. I have never labored to perpetuate the dominion of the bourgeoisie. On the contrary: I have always been preoccupied by the plight of the poor and the oppressed.

My first personal experience of poverty was this imprisonment. But it seems to me that the poor are born so and that it is almost impossible for us to cross class lines in the sense of escaping from our class consciousness. I realize that I live in a church that is rich and seems rich in the eyes of people. Even here in prison, whenever anyone needs anything, from an onion for soup to a hospital bed for a relative, they come looking for us priests. Priests, after all, have money, connections, prestige, power. We do what we can, but it is irritating to realize that this is the image of the church evoked by our presence. I wish we were the neediest of all, living witnesses to a poor church.

In my eyes poverty means putting yourself entirely at the service of the poor. If that seems very bourgeois, so be it! The important thing is that all my plans be directed to the effective liberation of the poor by effectual means. That is the poverty that I can and must live. I must be accountable to the disadvantaged and oppressed, not to the rich and powerful. It is the former who are the living image of Jesus Christ. The God I have come to know in the Bible is the God who liberates the poor and exalts them, who topples monarchs from their thrones and sends the rich away empty-handed.

This choice provokes the wrath of the rich. They are persecuting me because they will not allow anyone to destroy the evil they have set up. It is only natural that there should be conflict. (. . .) Prison has taught me to know freedom, has freed me from needing superfluous things, has freed me from the values that are part of the alienating machinery of the present social order. Goodbye to the myths of the bourgeoisie! Prison has reduced us to the plight of the poor by depriving us of our freedom, making us suffer, humiliating and traducing us, and leaving us completely at the mercy of others. This experience has taught me a lot. If the lessons I have learned survive the coming of freedom and its charms, then I will have succeeded in living the poverty I have chosen. I absolutely do not wish to return to the social class from which I came.

Now let's consider all this in the context of the religious life. Here we must do just a bit of theorizing, but I will simply tell you what I mean by the religious life. To begin with, the religious life antedates Christianity. The Essenes lived in monastic communities before the birth of Christ. Monasticism arose in the church about the fourth century, a time when the church was already allied with the Empire and Christianity was beginning to show signs of decadence. Persecution and martyrdom were things of the past. The group of Christians that would not accept concessions to the temporal power and wished to remain faithful to the inspiration of the church's first three centuries chose to live apart in the desert. There they were joined by fugitives from earlier persecutions. The communities they formed were intended to be the church's "final" witness. "Eschatology" is the word that defines the true meaning of the religious life, which arose as a *challenge* to the world.

As time went on the religious life became established and institutionalized and acquired formal rules; the poor monks of former times were replaced by rich abbots and lords of the manor. The cloisters no longer challenged the world, feeling that they had planted the kingdom of God on earth. The religious life proliferated and became so strong as to absorb the church itself, taking control of the hierarchy and the papacy. The cloister began to feel a desire to dominate the world. Attempts at renewal always consisted in establishing new forms of the same institution: Religious orders multiplied.

There was one clear call to radical change, but it proposed an idea whose time had not yet come and therefore went unanswered. Francis of Assisi came too soon: He will be understood by those who come after us. Francis did not wish to found a new order, much less an institution of the accustomed kind. He wanted to initiate a *movement* within the church of return to the gospel and to the poverty that should characterize it. But his successors betrayed him and destroyed his witness. Large and lofty monasteries replaced his bare shelters.

The religious life has continued to subsist on the margins of history. The last century saw a new flowering of religious foundations devoted to the philanthropies in which the church was beginning to engage: orders devoted to teaching, to hospital work, to the communications media.

What now? Without wishing to be a prophet, I predict the extinction of the institutional form of religious life. Our ranks will gradually empty; the membership of orders and congregations will progressively diminish. In their place I envision St. Francis's prophecy: movements within the church inspired to carry on a specific course of evangelical action without requiring their participants to live under the same roof or rule. These movements will comprise lay people, priests, nuns, and bishops. They will not have formal rules. This is how I envision the return to the gospel—not separate communities but movements originating within the church. (. . .) I am preparing myself for this new stage. It is already being born. (. . .)

105

To his parents

March 11

First a big hug for dad. Another year of life, another grandchild. (. . .) I'm sure the grandchild was the best present of all. Every time I see a child born, I realize more and more how good life is. The struggle for existence is hard but beautiful. I feel as if I were careening along in a sailboat, subject to every puff of wind on the sea of history. Sometimes I fall overboard, but it doesn't matter. I can swim. (. . .)

In between a book on theology and one on philosophy, I've read two interesting novels. The first was *One Day in the Life of Ivan Denisovich* by Solzhenitsyn. It is well worth reading. It's a brief and disturbing account of a situation much like mine. The subject of the other novel, by Ilya Ehrenburg, could not be more different: *Factory of Dreams* deals with the world of Hollywood movies, and what makes it interesting is the author's approach to his subject. He shows that the United States has been able to manufacture and export not only refrigerators, automobiles, soft drinks, and chewing gum but also illusions that have conditioned the lives and mentalities of countless moviegoers. (. . .)

A big hug to you all, especially to Dad, who is a real friend.

106

To a newborn baby girl[65]

March 29

Adriana, your grandpa has just left.[66] I was so moved and cheered by his visit that I could hardly talk. He seemed in great shape, with a spiritual and physical youthfulness that would be the envy of many people. I told him to give my love to your mama, Claudia, and to your aunts Vera and Maria Eugenia, just as if I were the brother they never had. How I envy your grandma Glaucia, who still swims in the pool! I've had enough of the Turkish baths we get here! . . . The snapshots your grandpa brought are great. You look like a typical newborn baby, all of whom look the same to me though to its parents each one is undeniably unique. Your mama's smile is a masterpiece of love.

In the darkness of the world I am thinking of you. I think that you have just been born for freedom and that you will spend your whole life seeking it. At some point you will discover that the key to freedom is love, and love has its stages. In the first stage we free ourselves by searching for someone to love, that is, we find *our* freedom in loving. Then we come to love so that others may be free. Finally we are willing not to be free so that others might be. You cannot understand this now, but life will teach you things that go beyond my words.

I pray for you. If what my body is suffering (though my spirit is joyful) can have any merit, then I ask the Lord to let this merit benefit you. God loves you so much that he wants you to take part in life, which is the best gift he can give. In the course of your life you too will wrestle with an angel. You will know times of doubt and times of certainty, times of discouragement and of courage, days of rain and days of sunshine. But you will prevail over the angel if you have faith in yourself, in others, and in God.

Adriana, I want you to be beautiful as a flower, pure and without vanity, genuine as the sun that does not ask permission to shine through prison bars. I want you to be strong as the rock from which flows the water that cleanses and quickens all that lives on earth. I want you to be patient as the butterfly, which turns beautiful inside its cocoon and does not fear the blowing of the wind as it flies. I want you to be brave as the sand on the beach, which does not fear the waves advancing to cover it. I wish you the faith of those who fight to win, the hope of those who bear the present in order to build the future, the love of those who do not fear to die because they know that love ends not in death but in rebirth.

All this I wish for you. I entrust you to the safety of your parents' arms. Today they carry you, tomorrow they may lean on you for support. That's the way life goes. Sometimes the road is tortuous and hard to follow, but that doesn't matter. The important thing is to keep alive inside us the meaning of the journey. If we can do this, we shine with an inner light that may blind others but can also awaken them.

To conclude my first letter to you, Adriana, I ask one thing of you: *Never forget the poor.* A big hug to papa Roberto and a kiss of peace and happiness to your mama and yourself. Peace and joy!

107

To Pedro

March 22

Dear Pedro, homesickness was beginning to get the better of me when your letter arrived. (. . .)

The prison world has led me to discover what lies back of and beneath reality. I've learned that beneath the rose petals are thorns, that beneath the broad avenues run refuse-laden sewers, that a tree that bears bitter fruit must be cut off at the roots. Neither medicine nor grafting will help it. The gospel tells us that we must cut it down and burn it. But how many people go on hoping for a harvest from a barren fig tree! When I think about your freedom to come and go, to attend theological meetings, to read and write, I must confess I envy you.

But I try at once to resist the feeling because I know that my place is not yours and that my contribution to God's plan is different from yours. (. . .)

Sometimes I'm afraid I won't be able to see this thing through because I feel theologically undernourished. What keeps me going is an immense, exaggerated confidence in divine providence; I cling to providence like one waiting for a miracle. But I know the nature and the risk of my own work, and I don't expect God to do it for me. I only ask him to help me do it well and to let my unending self-offering be meaningful and bear fruit.

During these sixteen months of imprisonment I have not yet lost my nerve. At no point have I felt that the past was useless or the future lost. On the contrary, I'm optimistic about both. For me this time in prison is a passage to liberation, a period of waiting for Easter. It counts as a second novitiate, in which I'm reaching a more profound understanding of the mystery embodied in Jesus of Nazareth. Now I know how false are any concepts of God that do not refer to the young man of Galilee. In him I find myself and define myself. But I do realize how ill prepared people are—even Christians—to hear and understand Jesus' summons. Not because his summons is complicated but precisely because it is too simple. It's difficult to come out of the labyrinth into which our traditional conditioning has led us. We aren't yet strong enough to face the temptations Jesus underwent in the desert. We adore temporal power, we look for security, and we fail to grasp how corrupting it is to bow down to the wielders of wealth and power. If we had Jesus' certainty that a legion of angels would come to our aid, we would not hesitate to cast ourselves from the hilltop. But we haven't this certainty, so we prefer to be a legal church rather than an evangelical, endangered church. Clearly the Holy Spirit is working to get the church moving. But I think we tempt him too much, always hoping for *him* to act. By the time he has acted too many sacrifices have already been consumed. He speaks to us primarily through events. It is events —sometimes tragic ones—that guide the church, though it would be better if the church guided events. It often seems to me that the church has an enormous capacity to pardon and absolve historical situations, but a glaring inability to initiate, advance, or prevent them. It's said that history is a good teacher. That may be, but human beings are poor students! God's intent moves toward fulfillment with or without the church and whether Christians like it or not. It's the history of salvation that is moving. As Teilhard de Chardin said, everything moves toward convergence despite detours and momentary reverses. Let us have faith; Easter is coming.

108

To his parents

April 6

(. . .) We're approaching Christianity's most important holy day: Easter. Saint Paul said that if Christ had not risen, our faith would be in vain. But he has risen, proving that death is not the end of life. The liberation proclaimed of old by the prophets came to pass in Jesus Christ, and the import of this fact is enormous. If Jesus had not been resurrected, then we could go on with life indifferently. We could eat and drink and dance, indifferent to all else, till death ended us and our revels together. But we believe that the young carpenter of Nazareth still lives in his Father's bosom and that we live and move by the power of his Spirit, and that changes everything. No one can ask me to live as if the resurrection had not been a critical event. The fulcrum of our earthly lives shifted in that moment when Christ conquered death. Since then anyone wanting to know why and for whom I live should try to understand the meaning of Christ's cross and resurrection rather than indulging in amazement at my seeming folly.

All this is easy to say but hard to carry out. If we believe —and establish our life on the belief—that resurrection, not death, is the end of earthly life, then it follows that nothing on earth is absolute. It is foolish to accumulate riches, to wrap oneself in prestige, to pile up guarantees, to attain a mediocre tranquillity. Probably these needs are so deeply rooted in our upbringing and our culture that we cannot easily relinquish them. But in Christ they are rendered absurd. He knows that the way to life leads through the cross. He saw in his death neither disgrace nor sorrow nor the frustration of all his purposes, but glorification: "The hour has come for the Son of Man to be glorified. In very truth I tell you, a grain of wheat remains a solitary grain unless it falls into the ground and dies; but if it dies, it bears a rich harvest. The man who loves himself is lost, but he who hates himself in this world will be kept safe for eternal life. If anyone serves me, he must follow me" (John 12:23–26).

Can a mother understand that her son was glorified precisely because his body was nailed on a cross between two thieves and would have been buried in a common grave but for the good will of Joseph of Arimathea? What could Mary have thought when she saw her son hunted, persecuted, imprisoned, beaten, and crucified? What mysterious glory was concealed in all that ignominy? Jesus was afraid. I know something of the fear that must have been his: "Now my soul is in turmoil, and what am I to say? Father, save me from this hour. No, it was for this that I came to this hour. Father, glorify thy name" (John 12:27–28). And his Father, as if wishing to infuse new strength into his Son, breaks the silence: "I have glorified it, and I will glorify it again" (John 12:28).

In the cross God revealed his inmost secret: his solidarity with the oppressed. The most incredible conversation in human history is the exchange between one of the thieves and Christ. Hanging on the cross, the thief acknowledges Jesus' innocence and asks: "Remember me when you come to your throne." He does not ask for a place in the kingdom or even to be saved; he simply asks to be remembered by someone. Jesus replies: "Today you shall be with me in Paradise." The first saint of the church is a thief condemned to death alongside Jesus.

Jesus' glorification is complete in his Resurrection. Now we know that we will preserve our lives if we are willing to lose them. We know that death no longer terrifies us. We also know that Jesus' innocence is suspect in the eyes of the world. What use is it for one convicted man to call another innocent? Yet by these dubious proceedings God brings liberation to humankind.

The prefiguration of Christ's Easter is the Exodus, the liberation of the Jews from bondage in Egypt. The God who reveals himself and leads his people through the wilderness is the same God who liberates this people and causes them to go on through human history. Through faith we are sure of Resurrection. In Easter we celebrate having been redeemed and saved in advance. We are the freest of human beings. All the barriers have been burst asunder.

But I wonder: Are we living like people who carry within themselves this certainty, who do not fear the painful aspect of this liberation brought by Christ, who are free enough to free others? We were challenged by Marxism a century ago, but it seems we have not yet succeeded in becoming a living image of the Resurrection. We are not yet wholly witnesses to Easter, artisans of liberation. We cling to life and reject death because we find it hard to believe that death too has its limits. We are still afraid of the cross, and we see no glory in Christ's sacrifice. He bore it for us, but we cannot bear it for him and for others. We still prefer the common sense of the world to the folly of the cross. We still strive to store up treasures on earth, though we know that in time to come they will not be worth one hair of our heads. The judgment of Caesar means more to us than the insight of the crucified thief.

But the most curious and tragic fact—our real challenge—is not that Christians lack the strength to inhabit a climate of Resurrection but that many non-Christians do inhabit such a climate, even though they do not believe that there is anything beyond the moment of giving up their lives. Surely these people are acting under the influence of grace. Their number grows every day, as if they were living the word of God even without believing in it.

Here we are trying to prepare for Easter by meditating on the relationship between Cross and Resurrection. Prison gives special meaning to our liturgical life. It puts us in direct touch with the passion of Christ because it makes us participants in his agony. But it also leads us to believe even more strongly in the reality of Easter. (. . .)

Archbishop Evaristo[67] has returned from Europe and is supposed to visit us one of these days. He may celebrate Easter Mass here in Tiradentes Prison. Father Torrini[68] is going from cell to cell, preparing the prisoners. Giulio[69] will be here for another two months even though his lawyer appealed his sentence. Maybe you've read in the newspapers that we've asked to be freed on bail.[70] But it wouldn't be soon even if they granted it. Laercio[71] appealed last September, and he will be finishing his sentence this coming May. The Superior Military Tribunal moves slowly because it has too many cases to handle.

I'm pleased that Dad is reading Mounier. There was a time when his books influenced me greatly. I read everything of his that I could lay my hands on, and from him I learned the meaning of Christian commitment. Happy Easter and a big hug to you all.

109

To his sister Cecilia

May 12

Dearest Cecilia, I would so love to spend your birthday with you and your little family. (. . .)

When we are imprisoned and unable to embrace those we most love, the roots of love grow painful in our hearts. There are bars separating us, and hands like ours made and set in place these bars that keep our hands from touching.

My love for you is as great as the distance that separates us. Something in your simplicity and silence has always moved me deeply. You are one of those rare people who are always familiar with poverty and therefore have great inner riches. Many things in you correspond to my image of Mary. Perhaps

177

it's because you don't have to make any effort to love God. He loves you, and your life shows it.

My relationship with God is very different from yours. I live in constant struggle with him. I get angry and argue with him; I am never satisfied. You, on the other hand, are at peace with him. Like Mary, you have been wise enough to say, "Be it done unto me according to thy will," and to leave the rest to him. When I was still very young, God tore me from my family, laid a heavy yoke across my shoulders, and sent me to live among strangers in a strange land. Of you he demanded nothing exceptional. He laid no yoke on you, nor did he tear you from your family. I resisted him, but he won and compelled me to a vocation I never thought I had. You, however, seem never to have resisted him, and he has always been your neighbor, your confidant, and your friend.

It's been different with me. There have been times when he has shaken me to the depths. There have been times when he has been silent and I couldn't find him anywhere. There have been times when his silence so enraged me that I threatened to abandon him. But he's used to my temper and has never taken my threats seriously. You he has let go your own ordinary, uneventful way, undistinguished except by the love that is reborn in you each day.

But look what he has done to me: He has led me from place to place; he has let me make good friends and then taken me from them; he has led me in strange paths, made me front-page news, and brought me in the end to this prison.

Sometimes I ask: How long, O Lord? And I think he is not yet done with demanding of me much more than I can possibly give.

There are days when I have remained standing only because he willed it. If it had depended on my own strength I would have fallen a thousand times. In my heart of hearts I ask God to let me be like you: peaceful and possessed of a faith as transparent as a mountain stream. But it's no use! He wills me to live amid storms and tempests, so I must cling to the thread of faith that he grants me.

Cecilia, the real tragedy is that God trusts too much in us. He wants us to be his presence among people. Sometimes I imagine what it must be like to be pope—head of the church of Jesus Christ on earth! Who are we? What are we capable of?

You have been wise enough to entrust yourself to him and let him act in you. Not me. I always want to anticipate him. I don't have your calm. I'm always in a hurry, always wanting to do something. And after I've rushed into something, God comes and tells me that it's not exactly what he had in mind. Then I must start over from the beginning, changing the plans and putting in more work. Does he think I have your infinite patience?

I imagine your prayer as being wholly silent. You tell God you love him, and God replies that he loves you even more. I don't pray. I debate. When I pray, I propose a set of problems, ask for solutions, propose tentative solutions of my own, analyze, argue. . . . There are days when I feel he doesn't even want to listen to me, but I keep talking. I ask for something, he gives me something else; I imply something, he infers something else. Perhaps it will go on like that till we meet face to face. . . . Then we'll come at last to an understanding.

I was thinking about sending you a gift, but you've already received the best possible gift—your son. By the time I get to meet him, he probably won't be a baby any more. I remember something that happened when you were teaching slum kids. On Teacher's Day the students brought you gifts, and the poorest of them, the child of a candy peddler, gave you a tiny jar of guava jam that his father had given him. It was the most beautiful gift of all. I'm in the same spot now as that little boy was then. I can't buy you anything, so I'm sending you something I made with my own hands—a necklace of glass beads, like the one I gave Teresa. Mom told me that you all liked hers.

A big hug to your husband, whom I like. A kiss for the baby. And to you all my love.

110

May 12

Dear Pedro, Ivo's solemn profession of vows was an immensely important event for us. The setting couldn't have been more meaningful: Some wooden planks that usually serve as our writing desk and kitchen table on that day became the altar.

After a year and a half of "retreat," he was more than prepared. I should like to be ordained a priest here because here I have become the one who sacrifices and is sacrificed. Will I be granted that grace? The fact is that I have already been granted it. As Ignatius of Antioch said, we can consecrate bread and we can turn ourselves into living bread. Priesthood as charisma, in the profoundest sense of the word, is far more than a set of churchly functions. Here this is the common priesthood. Priesthood as a function within the ecclesial community exists only to the extent that it is at once the expression and result of a life of giving, of service, and of witness. A person who simply "conducts services" has not yet discovered the true dimensions of the priesthood. Body and blood are something much more real than "services," don't you think? What is the use of daily re-enacting Christ's sacrifice if we don't undertake it in our own lives? Dear friend, it's not very disturbing to deal with soul and spirit and mind; it's only when one deals with body and blood that the fear and trembling begin. We are capable of living for the gospel, but are we capable of dying for the gospel?

I see that you have great plans for study. Here, lacking books, we extract our lessons from our daily lives. I envy you because I've always wanted to study methodically, but reality shattered that dream. So I can only write letters, but even that is something. I've made up a thousand study plans, but they all come to nothing. I've managed to study a little theology, philosophy, and economics (not thoroughly—I just read the books I can get). It's the least one needs to know in order to decipher the complex reality in which we live.

I see you have managed to free yourself of the label "scholar." "Exegesis as a discipline of interpretation" is precisely what we need. What good does it do to read the Bible if we can't apply it to concrete contemporary events? (. . .)

It's almost unbelievable how many churchmen live in a vacuum, isolated in their own utopia. They don't know where Laos is, who the prime minister of Israel is, how much a liter of milk costs, what the average salary is in their part of the country, or what social and health services are available. They don't look for causes, they never ask why, they take poverty and wealth for granted, they find war scarcely objectionable, and they are convinced that good will, patience, and prudence will remedy all ills. How are we to preach the gospel to people who look upon us as aliens, who don't understand our language, to whom we represent another class and a different world?

You sent me a poem, so I will send you a story. There was a family of small farmers, poor and religious. One son went into the seminary. At night the mother in her naiveté dreamed that her son would come home a bishop, clad all in red, admired and honored by all the rich landowners who lived in town. From the seminary the boy wrote to his sister, the only one in the family who could read and write. In the evening she read his letters aloud by candlelight. He always wrote about the same things: the athletics at the seminary, roast-chicken dinners on Sunday, classes in Latin and Greek and history. He told them that he had the whole day to study, that he could see movies on the weekend, and that the liturgical feasts were beautifully celebrated at the seminary. In the evenings his parents would thank the Lord for the good fortune that had befallen their son. He had been freed from the bondage of the hoe, he had shelter from the rain, and even in times of drought he could be sure of a good meal. One day the son returned home for his vacation. His parents killed the fattest hog and the tenderest cow and barbecued them. They even managed to find a nice mattress for him. But when the whole family got up at dawn to go to the fields, he stayed home in bed. While his brothers were hoeing the stony ground, he was bent over his books. In those books, thought his family, was all the knowledge in the world. His brothers didn't have the courage to address a word to him because they were ashamed of their ignorance. His mother noticed that her son had difficulty in drinking the well water and that his feet were so smooth he could no longer walk barefoot over the earth that gave them sustenance. When he spoke, everyone listened with awed respect. No one replied or offered ideas. They knew that his life was "over there," on the other side of the mountain, in the big city where the seminary was located. When vacation was over, the boy left his home and went back to his studies. He left behind in his parents' poor cottage neither longing nor sadness—only the certainty that this son who had left them to enter God's house would never come home again. (. . .)

111

To a student friend

May 13

Dear Paulo, I am delighted to be in touch with you again. I like talking to you because you're the kind who is always thinking about things and looking for solutions, like me. Here, of course, there is too much time for thinking and rethinking everything. In prison you acquire a more comprehensive view of historical events. Out of the game and sitting on the bench, you can better observe the plays of those still on the field. The very fact of being shut in—we get out of the cell only five hours a week—prompts questions and discoveries we would never have dreamed of before. It's a centripetal process, yet it never degenerates into mere subjectivism. This is no place for contemplating your navel. A prisoner is always in the company of others, and that forces him to reveal himself for what he really is. The demand for objectivity is constant, and this results in stripping away all bourgeois falseness of feeling.

It's a situation that can humanize a person or dehumanize him. Just try to lock up a few rats together in a box: They will destroy and devour each other. When people are locked up together, there is always the same danger, but it never happens among political prisoners. Just the opposite occurs, in fact: People become humanized to an amazing degree. Once the individual has no recourse to flight, isolation, or fantasy, he is constrained to confront himself in the process of confronting others. He is constrained to think, to assess his own limits and those of others. Living together day after day gives rise to profound fellowship, to the ability to live together all day every day, to the discovery of self and other in the context of mutual relationship. In this barred world externals don't count; all that matters is what you are. What are social position, family tradition, or cultural level worth if the thing that saves you is your openness to others? The one who suffers here is the person who is incapable of being simple, relaxed, openhearted, and friendly.

The metamorphosis in some prisoners is astounding. They arrive here with class delusions intact, but gradually they lose interest in pretense and reveal themselves in a surprising way. They cease pretending and posturing and adapt to the prison lifestyle, which in other circumstances might lead to total brutalization. Only our endurance, our inner strength, enables us to live with dignity in prison.

Sometimes I think that this is the ideal we have not managed to attain in our religious communities, namely, an integration that demands the total and unreserved personalization of each individual. In our religious communities we get just the opposite. In the name of an integration that is purely juridical, the individual gives up his own personality. Such deception is possible only so long as we cling to "our own" lives, "our own" friendships, "our own" interests, "our own" rooms. When we can no longer turn back, when everything necessarily belongs to "the other," then very few things are "ours," and this really is community life. You learn to be responsible for yourself and for others. I've lived in a cell with forty people of the most widely differing backgrounds, upbringing, and educations. We formed ourselves into groups, each with an assigned task—cooking, cleaning, recreation, study. The system worked fine; we had no need of anyone to give orders. That was because any one person's failure to do his share would inevitably hurt the whole community. When one can withdraw (or shirk) without the community's noticing it, then there is no longer a community, just a group of individuals who share nothing but the fact that they live under the same roof. (. . .)

I ask your prayers for all those living their passion here. In one way or another they all hope in the resurrection. I know that the freely given love of our heavenly Father is not to be measured by our yardsticks. A big, affectionate hug to you.

112

To Pedro

May 16

Dear Pedro, I have just now finished reading *Octogesima Adveniens*.[72] I notice myself becoming increasingly demanding by comparison to the teachings of the church. The root of my severity and my impatience is a profound and passionate love for the church. I want to see the church free and untainted and poor—at one with its founder. If I note errors in this latest document, I don't blame them on the pope but rather on the limitations inherent in his function under contemporary circumstances.

Certainly, you can see advances in this document—in certain respects surprising advances. For example, the document criticizes democracy and accepts a socialism that safeguards the values guaranteeing integral human development, especially liberty, responsibility, and openness to the spiritual (no. 31). But I cannot accept certain flaws that keep showing up in documents of this sort and turn them into two-edged swords.

One clear advance is the fact that no one is arguing about

words any more. Remember the publication of *Mater et Magistra?* Everyone wanted to know exactly how the Latin should be translated. Now the terms are clear-cut and unambiguous—though their *practical import* for the pope may still be unclear. Just a short few years ago the word "socialism" sounded like blasphemy to Christian ears. How times change!

Octogesima Adveniens presents a well-thought-out list of world problems, though with certain inexplicable limitations. It is written by a European for Europeans. Once again you get the impression that the universality of the church is confined to western Europe and the rest of the world is heathen territory still to be converted. Not a word about war or the arms race, and only a glancing reference, in comparative terms, to the dizzying escalation of military expenditures.

Obviously it isn't possible to broach every problem in one document. But the principal ones certainly should be tackled. This document talks about the problems as if they were simply "abuses" of a social order that in itself is quite natural and Christian. . . . I suspect Pope Paul prefers a country where contemplative monasteries and pornography fairs stand side by side (I can hear him say, "At least they have freedom there!") to one where such contrasts are less glaring and human dignity is more respected but Western religions are regarded with a certain coolness.

On the other hand, this document does suggest that a new social order is justified because no existing model is "completely satisfactory." The author's analytic methodology seems defective. He can list the surface manifestations of problems, but he never gets down to their historical causes. How are we to overcome these problems? Must we simply wait for those in power to undergo some sort of conversion? This is the most dangerous element of utopianism in the church's teaching. It doesn't seem to me that Jesus directed his apostles to the religious and political leaders of their day. Instead he himself turned to the poor and tried to initiate a dialogue with them. One positive feature of *Octogesima Adveniens* is its recognition that there can be no one, universally valid solution and that some decisions properly rest with the local churches. This decentralization will benefit the church because experience has shown that imported official solutions only exacerbate problems.

The pope states that "it is the role of each Christian community to analyze objectively the situation in its own country and elucidate it in the light of the Gospel" (no. 4). This increases the responsibility of the rest of us; we may no longer wait for Rome to speak before we act. It is not the pope who will tell the churches of Haiti, Senegal, or the Philippines what to do, but the Christians who live in these countries. The same faith can lead different people to different undertakings (see *Gaudium et Spes,* no. 43). But none of these undertakings may contradict Jesus' meaning in proclaiming the good news to the poor.

The condemnation of liberalism in *Octogesima Adveniens* also represents a step forward: "Philosophical liberalism is at its very root a false affirmation of individual autonomy in action and motive as well as in the exercise of freedom" (no. 35). We have lived so long under this ideology that it has even contaminated church doctrine. Incredible that it has taken us until now to realize how antievangelical it is. We are still not aware of all the mischief wreaked by liberalism. Section no. 18 clearly reveals the author's belief that, serious problems notwithstanding, the existing system incorporates "a general movement of solidarity, through an effective policy of investment and of organization of trade and commerce, as well as of education." He still believes that the members of international organizations are capable of suiting their actions to their words.

This is the most difficult point to accept. International organizations such as NATO and the International Monetary Fund unilaterally serve the interests of the stronger nations that control them. They do not accept pluralism at all. Small nations that refuse to play the game by the rules of the game are shoved to the sidelines. An orange tree cannot bear apples. If we want apples, we must create conditions in which apples can be produced.

In short this document does not tackle the etiology of the

problems. Along with ingenious analysis it offers unfounded assertions like the following statement that "certain ideologies produce nothing but a change in masters who, while their power lasts, envelop themselves in privilege, restrict the freedom of others, and establish new forms of injustice." There are places where this has actually happened, but the document does not name them; nor does it say what conditions obtained in these places before the changes occurred. For the most part these changes are to the people's advantage, but one cannot compare the newly established orders with corrupt and decadent liberal societies. (. . .)

It is worth noting that the author addresses himself to Christians in general, never to Catholics in particular. But how does he think of the church? In his own words: "In some places they [Christians] are reduced to silence and regarded with suspicion [totalitarian societies]; in others they constitute a weak, scarcely noticeable minority. In yet others the church's position is recognized—or even officially established." I get the feeling that the author judges the last-named situation to be the most fitting. Naturally we should hope for complete freedom to preach and practice Christianity. But the most convenient situation is not always the most evangelical. We are in grave danger of making convenience our criterion. In many countries the church's position is recognized but at the price of its silence. The price is too high. The church must walk the road of poverty and persecution—so *Lumen Gentium* tells us, but we don't seem too convinced. We regard poverty as a heavy yoke and persecution as a disgrace that limits our freedom. That which is truly grace we regard as misfortune or disaster. We have fallen into opportunism and have lost the meaning of the gospel. We are not ready for poverty and persecution. Do we really trust in the Holy Spirit, in the Lord's promise to be with us always? What does it matter if our position is not recognized, if we become—again—a "tiny remnant"? God has need of us so that human beings may come to know him, but he does not need us to save them. The gratuitousness of his love transcends all our efforts.

Section 48 is the one that alarmed me the most. The author

187

implicitly confesses what was previously admitted by Pius XII, namely, that we have lost the working class. In other words the pope is aware that the church is enmeshed in the bourgeoisie. By saying that the church "has sent priests on an apostolic mission to the working class," the pope raises the question: *Where was the Church* when it sent these priests? Where else but among the rich? But matters should have been exactly opposite. We should have sent worker-priests to the bourgeoisie. We should be rooted in the world of the poor. Then we would not be required to pass through the eye of the needle to attain salvation.

There are, finally, two passages I should like to cite in order to convey two of my fundamental principles. The first is in section 36: "In serving his fellow-men the Christian must —without allowing himself to be compromised by any system—endeavor to reveal through his choices the specifically Christian contribution to the transformation of society." I would change it to read: "In serving his fellow-men the Christian must—while questioning all systems—. . . . "

The second passage occurs in section 48: "It is not enough to recall precepts, to state intentions, to note crying injustices, and to intone prophetic denunciations. It is all empty talk unless accompanied—on the part of every Christian—by intense awareness of personal responsibility and by effective action." As was said at the Medellín Conference,[73] the present still has time for words, but it is swiftly becoming a time for action.

There are other comments I would like to make but can't in the present context. Underlying this critical examination is a great love for the church. I do not want it to be, like a prostitute, the tool of anyone who can pay. I want it to be the image of Jesus Christ.

All of us in here send a big hug to all of you out there. Let us remain united in the Holy Spirit, who has made the cross a signpost on the road toward the future.

113

May 17

Dear Luciano, if you only knew how much Mom admires you and likes you. . . . When I read her description of you, I felt as though I'd known you for a long time.

Your letter is a little embarrassing. It makes me sound as though I'm not made of flesh and bone at all (in reality I think I'm more flesh than bone). If my witness—as God has permitted me to bear witness—has such impact on people, it's because the church is in bad shape. We should be the rule, not the exception. We are simply living according to the gospel and taking all the consequences. When Jesus warned his disciples that they would face many hardships, he didn't consider it a tragedy. The tragedy is elsewhere, in an established, officially recognized church that calls to mind a feudal aristocracy more than a manger in Bethlehem. The tragedy lies in the realization that God's word no longer rouses and converts but is restricted to alleviating the sufferings of the poor and justifying the egotism of the rich. (. . .)

I have never wanted to be a prisoner, just as Jesus never wanted the cup that was given him to drink. But since I find myself here, I want to put the occasion to good use. Human wickedness does not limit God's plan. In this place I've had a chance to see the other side of the coin, to deepen my aims, and to renew my conversion. I know my weaknesses, my limits and defects, but now I know that suffering does not destroy me, human and vulnerable though I am, that prison doesn't snuff out freedom, that darkness does not shut out my light, and that death will bring me to resurrection. Now I know what the parable of the sower and the seeds means.

I've learned a lot here, primarily that we discover our true selves only when we are confronted by our own limits. The animal pursued by a hunter measures its own strength. Look at the story of Job. Although he didn't know God's plan, he didn't despair. He trusted, and his hope was rewarded.

Why is the church so upset when its possessions are threatened? Why do we fear poverty and persecution? Why are we so afraid that the church's image might suffer? If the church doesn't communicate Jesus Christ, then it ought to be not just disfigured but destroyed. Unfortunately such changes are more often forced upon us by circumstances than freely embraced by us for the sake of the gospel. But the changes will come. Very soon we will forget our own personal problems and commit ourselves to something very different.

Luciano, I hope to be able to continue this newly begun dialogue with you. I know that in my house they like you very much. Take my place at table. Some day we will be together to celebrate our deepening friendship.

114

To his sister Cecilia

May 19

(. . .) Here they are suspicious even of our breathing. The food that is sent to us every week is inspected minutely and maliciously. (. . .) Countless little humiliations are repeated every day. You'll get an idea of what it's like if you think back to when we were little kids and the grownups were always saying, "Stop that! What have you got in your hand? Beat it!"

That's the kind of thing that goes on here, and it's not easy to take when you're over twenty-one (some of us are over forty). The poor slobs who guard us have gotten a raw deal in life. They are treated like dirt by their superiors, and they take out their rage on us.

If one has not had a certain upbringing and therefore lacks a certain point of view, as is the case with most of the nonpolitical prisoners, all that bad treatment leads to silent revolt. That is the source of the brawls that break out almost daily among the nonpolitical prisoners. It is their only way of shaking off the humiliations put upon them. The political prisoners, on the other hand, never lose their heads and can demand and get more dignified treatment, though it's not easy when you're dealing with a guard who comes to work half-drunk and worried to death about his unpaid bills.

The life we live and the tragedies we witness can only be understood by someone who has been here. At night terrible shrieks break the heavy silence of people who by now are accustomed to feeling powerless and showing no reaction to anything. A prisoner howls and howls, or cries like a baby, and when you ask the guard what's going on he says that someone has gone crazy or that there was a fight in the cell. It's also possible that the prisoner in question has been tortured. But there are frequent cases of madness here, and last month there was another suicide. A prisoner tied his pants to the window-bars, looped them around his neck, and then jumped as hard as he could (because the cell windows are not that high). Like the other suicides that have happened here, the whole affair remains shrouded in mystery. No one knows where his cell-mates were or where the guards were. No one saw anything. No one says anything.

In the beginning such things bothered me terribly. In time I learned that someone living in the jungle cannot afford to be afraid of snakes.

If in one way I have become thick-skinned, like the grave-digger who earns his living from the dead, in another I have learned to direct all these experiences into a profound and continued conversion, by which my faith and my ideals become greater and purer. I see our little problems of the outside world for the molehills they really are. Some of our bourgeois concerns are completely silly and out of place. Human reality is very serious, and we privileged souls must not permit ourselves to live apart from other people's sufferings. We must reach their suffering and eradicate it.

I hope to be a guest in your new home. May it be as simple and hospitable as you are.

115

May 25

Dear Cousin, when I read your letters I realize that you and I think alike about the Christian life and that we two experience with particular intensity the mystery of the cross and of joy. I am becoming more and more convinced that it is really a privilege to live in this postconciliar period of church history, in which we are required to play a responsible part in the process of renewal. But the renewal will come from below, from prophets, not from experts in canon law, from those open to the future rather than those attached to the past. Our excessive attachment to juridical values—a hallmark of the Western mind—has too often caused us to forget that the human person is a being in continual evolution, capable of transforming and being transformed, full of questions that are infinite in scope and that only faith can answer. We often take refuge in the status quo, believing that the present is definitive and unchangeable. But in reality, if we don't prepare ourselves to face the cyclone that is devastating our age and driving it toward an unknown future, we are in danger of running aground on the myths and utopias of the present.

The same phenomenon occurred in the fifteenth and sixteenth centuries, when human creativity overcame many barriers that till then had seemed insurmountable. Navigation and international trade broke down the barriers between peoples and enlarged geographical confines. Technology and science increased man's dominion over himself and nature. Philosophical subjectivism turned the universal order upside down and made man the center and the measure of all things. All barriers crumbled—economic, social, artistic, political, and religious—and the world grew wider. Man felt somehow insecure and lost in its immensity. Many people thought it was the end of everything, when in fact it was the beginning of a new era.

Today we are living through a similar situation. The moon,

once a symbol of romance or madness, is now a real place on which human beings have walked.

How will we go about reconciling our old values with the new world of space, the progress of automation, artificial insemination, the dizzying rate of scientific advances, and the capacity to probe the deepest mysteries of the universe? Everything familiar seems to be crumbling around us while these new realities seem to be infinite in dimension and absolute in their power. The cyclone raging around us for the last few decades has shaken not only the outside world but also the foundations of our inner world. Moral and religious barriers have toppled, and the younger generation has launched itself on a frantic search, looking everywhere and not finding much. Atheism is a collective phenomenon; sex is a commercially furnished diversion and very profitable; earning-power becomes the supreme criterion of professional achievement. At the same time contradictions multiply: We talk a great deal about peace and live amid wars; poverty and wealth live side by side.

Clearly these convulsions will end sooner or later, even if we don't know when or how. A Christian cannot be pessimistic about the future. These are the pangs of childbirth that bring a new world, a new promised land that is our journey's end. It is the goal we seek, but like Moses we will probably never set foot in it.

What, then, should be the attitude of the church toward a materialistic, unbelieving, and exploitative world in possession of scientific knowledge that challenges our religious faith? Should we go into the desert and wait there apart till the storm subsides? Should we abandon our faith and plunge into the whirlpool of a world in turmoil? Surely these are not the only two alternatives open to us. We can no longer barricade ourselves inside the church, praying and doing penance on behalf of the "outside world." Our vision must be based not on despair but on faith.

How does God see the world? This may seem like a rhetorical question, but for me it is a radical and basic problem. The Bible tells me that the Lord is not only involved in human history but also reveals himself through this history. I open the newspaper to read the plans of God. Every human action, wherever it may take place, is an act of salvation or perdition. The criterion of judgment is easy enough, and it is provided by the gospel: We are saved when we are willing to lose ourselves for others, but we are truly lost when we are concerned solely with our own salvation. So I think God sees the world very clearly. He does not experience crises as we do because he knows that his kingdom is eschatological. We have crises because we forget this fact and concentrate all our hope on the present or live nostalgically in the past. If human beings seem to us to be moving farther away from God because they are abandoning the church, it is because we confuse the church with God. I think that human beings are seeking God more anxiously than ever before. If they withdraw from the church, the fault is ours because we bear witness to a god of nationhood and private property who no longer chooses to suffer on the cross, to a god who is not the God of Jesus Christ. If a world in turmoil frightens us, what kind of leaven do we propose to be?

It should be crystal clear to us Christians that our task is not to judge the world. Our mission is to save it. Or rather, *human beings will be saved by the gratuitous gift of God's love, which is the essence of our proclamation.* This being the case, how can we think that human beings are far removed from God? The very fact of being a human being in the world is a blessing from God. Hence I think that human beings are imbued with the values of the gospel, eager for love, and full of hope, even though they do not recognize the revelation of Jesus Christ as the expression of the foundations of their existence.

There is sin, it is true. But it is also true that grace is stronger than sin. God looks upon the world with love and confidence and therefore so must we.

Sometimes events trouble us. Discouragement overtakes us, and the feeling that anything we might do would be absolutely useless. Who is mistaken, we or the world? I always prefer to think that it is we who are mistaken. We have been well trained to teach catechism to children according to the

Tridentine formulas, according to medieval theology and neo-platonic philosophy. We are locked into an illusionary spirituality and becalmed amid aristocratic institutions. If we cannot renew ourselves, we will never understand the nature and scope of the changes that the world is going through. The gospel says that we are to be the leaven of the world, not its image, but we succumb to the temptation to be image and not leaven. The shape that the world may take in a particular age is not important for us. Our concern is to be truly its leaven, utilizing everything we have learned from our faith. Mystical experience should help us to recognize the presence of God, not only in our own lives but in the lives of all people and in the evolution of the universe. (. . .)

Today we had the pleasure of saying goodbye to Father Giulio Vicini, who was released after serving four months of his sentence.[74] Now there are three of us in this cell.

A hug to you and your sisters. Much friendship.

116

To Sister Alberta, a Brazilian nun

June 17

Dear Sister Alberta, your postcard was a welcome surprise because I have always esteemed your faith and your vocation. I know that you can understand what we are feeling and living through here precisely because of that faith and vocation. (. . .)

The judge has personally assured us that we will come to trial in July. It does not seem likely to us, however, even though the progress of our case has picked up in the last few months. On the first of June we learned that our request to be freed on bail under house arrest had been denied. From that fact we gather that we will be sentenced to at least two years. It's ridiculous, but there is nothing to be done. Now we are hoping that the Supreme Military Tribunal will okay our appeal. It's a matter of waiting. No suffering, no privation is eternal.

There are now three of us in this cell. We are neither resigned to our fate nor despairing. We try to understand it in the light of faith, to explore the possible import of such an event in the life of a Christian. In this respect we can say that ours is a privileged situation, one that furthers our efforts toward a lasting conversion to Jesus Christ. This does not mean that coercion acts upon us as a tranquillizer; rather, it enables us to see more clearly that our situation and our actions can have a positive impact on the life of the church. If it did not, rebellion—or despair—would be inevitable.

But when we realize that the fact of our presence here is a sign of the church's vitality, then all we need do is give ourselves up wholly to the Lord's intentions. This is not vanity. On the contrary, we are aware of a great responsibility—the responsibility and humility of the sown seed, the fidelity of the useless servant. Neither conscience nor the church nor God accuses us. So why should we fear "the wisdom of the world" when we know that our redemption rests in "the folly of the cross?"

My companions and I thank you for your words of friendship and support. We entrust ourselves to your prayers and promise to pray for you. Peace to you all.

117

To Liana, a friend

June 20

When I read your letters, Liana, I feel as if they had been written by an angel. They breathe pure-heartedness. You scarcely seem to be flesh and blood at all. The only hitch is that you call me "holier" (?) than yourself. That's a real joke! If you only knew how much I have to grow! Besides, the traditional image of the saint does not appeal to me at all. . . . I prefer to have my feet on the ground, to be human among humans, to participate in life. I know that you do the same because you work and keep up friendships outside the limited circle of your own church. If you want to be leaven in the dough, there is no point in staying inside the package.

I don't know very much about the structure or history of your church. You will have to explain it to me. As far as my own church is concerned, it will have to make an about face before it can become leaven in the dough. The story of the Catholic church is very similar to that of the monk who forsook his land and goods to go into the desert and live a life of strict poverty. Since he was cold and a little ill he accepted heavy clothing from a friend who came to visit. As time went on, he was surrounded by an ever-increasing multitude who came to venerate him and to express their gratitude and leave gifts in exchange for favors received through his intercession. The monk replaced his bowl with a plate, ate with a spoon instead of his fingers, put boots on his bare feet, and left the cave and the hard ground for a dry dwelling and soft bed.

To the people who began to voice a suspicion that he was no longer poor, the monk replied, "Just gifts! Simply gifts!" His possessions (to which he claimed he was "unattached") mounted, and he had cultivated land and plenty of food to eat. Eventually he produced more than he needed and began to sell the surplus. Concerned over the growing number of his disciples, he had a large monastery built to house them. This monastery was in all respects like the fief of a feudal lord. It produced the best wine in the area, as well as a great many other things that the monks sold. Everyone praised the monastery's prosperity, kings acknowledged its economic importance, and the monk who had founded it became a veritable prince. He was given, among other things, a title of nobility.

But the monks continued to take vows of poverty and to tell the poor, "You are the Lord's favorites." They praised the poverty of the Servant of Yahweh and were convinced that, despite the wealth of monastery and fief all around them, none of it was actually "theirs." Since it didn't belong to the poor either, the monks insisted that "it all belonged to the church and to God." It was God and the church who made sure that the monks had bread and wine everyday, while outside the monastery the poor went hungry and consoled themselves by thinking of the poverty of Christ, whose minister and representatives on earth the monks felt themselves to be.

What am I to do? How can I preach what I do not live? How can I teach what I do not do? I am a liar because I do not bear witness to what I proclaim. I am full of false pride because I wish to be taken for what I am not. It is the old schism between faith and witness, theory and practice, ideals and life.

Today the church is aware of this problem. Vatican II represented an effort to pinpoint and overcome the causes of this schism but we still have a long way to go. In theory many things have already been accomplished: We have rediscovered the Bible, we have formulated a new definition of the church as the people of God, we have perceived that God is present in human history, we have reformed the liturgy and entrusted tasks to the laity, we have come to esteem poverty as an essential precondition for apostolic work, we have acknowledged the autonomy of the temporal world and the service to humanity that the Church must undertake. And there are attempts to move from theory to practice.

But to practice what we profess we must break with the past. Once and for all the church must renounce its privileged position in society. It may not be a church *for* the poor; it must be a church *of* the poor. If the rich wish to enter this church they must pass through the eye of the needle.

Whenever you can, tell me about the problems of your church. Probably they are different from ours. But we do have much in common: faith in the same God and a desire to save the same world. As far as I know, your church retains the characteristics of its country of origin. This is true of us too. We have tried to force the Catholic church into a Roman mold, even in countries that have no connection with Western civilization. Today we see the error in that, and we are trying to remedy it.

I think that our common religious concerns can serve as a basis for dialogue. We should exchange ideas on our experiences. Thus we can help each other to be more authentic.

Here life goes on as usual: iron bars and not much sunshine. But we feel the serenity of knowing that all this has meaning even if it is slow to bear fruit. It seems absolutely certain that we will not get out of here before the end of the year.

We pray for your apostolate, offering up our sufferings that you may be successful and grow in faith, hope, and love. Fernando, Ivo, and I send you a big hug and all our love.

118

To Marlene, a friend

June 20

Marlene, your letter, which I've read twice from beginning to end, is very human and as beautiful as the sunflowers you have planted on your farm. It is like you. To be in touch with the earth is a good thing. Here I miss it very much. It's been quite a while since I've seen fields, or anything green—my landscape is all cement and iron. It's an oppressive panorama. I miss the open air and the vistas in which you can lose yourself. . . . I was born in the mountains and spent my first years on the seacoast. My earliest memory of myself is that of a small boy playing with a little pail on the Copacabana beach. That was when I was three or four, and it's my only memory of that time—the rest is gone. This has stayed with me because I love the sea above anything else in nature. It frightens me and consoles me at the same time because it hides a mysterious richness.

There is another spectacle I never tire of contemplating: human beings. What could be more beautiful or more terrible? People can cultivate roses, write poetry, compose music—and they can also make weapons of war, oppress each other, and condemn each other to death. We have a long way to go to recapture the unity described in the first chapter of Genesis. Right now we are a mass of contradictions, undoubtedly because we are self-deceived.

One of the most important moments of my life came when I realized that my existence had a social dimension. Only then did I begin to grasp its personal dimension. Until that moment I had believed in the law of the jungle, in which competition, not cooperation, was the key. I left off competing in order to cooperate. I ceased wanting so that I would be able to choose. It suddenly came to me that every choice entails a renunciation. You cannot flutter through life from one possibility to the next without ever committing yourself to any. Choosing one path at a crossroads necessarily excludes the others. At times you are overtaken by the temptation to turn back or take dubious shortcuts that at first glance seem easier but always turn out more tortuous. You must keep going, patiently and determinedly, trusting your own legs and nurturing your hope in the destination that awaits you.

The things we have been taught don't emphasize the social dimension of human existence. . . . I learned to read and write from the Uncle Paperone books. I piously believed that one day I would be as rich as he. I spent my childhood with Captain Marvel and Zorro. My heroes were strong men, and they won with force. I could sleep in peace because they would protect me. . . . The enemies of my heroes—the outlaws, thugs, and trouble-makers—looked a little bit like Mexicans. All these books taught me that crime doesn't pay, but also that it was no crime to make money. They also taught me that the ideal man, the prototype of virility, was super-fed, super-equipped, and super-envied. I learned that I must become one of them at all costs, and I dreamed of my future as I chewed gum and drank Coke. I had a passionate admiration for Uncle Sam.

My sensibilities were further developed by the movies. They continued the education that my comic books began, reinforcing the same values vividly and crudely. They taught me that love is a pretty face and a nice figure, and that I would have to plunge headfirst into incredible adventures in order to be a real man. From the movie screen I learned a whole host of things that no one would have the courage to teach anyone in real life. The fulfilled man was rich, clean-shaven, stylishly dressed, successful with women, and surrounded by flunkies who jumped to satisfy his every whim. When I left the movie house, I was convinced that my own life would duplicate in every respect what I saw on the screen, provided that I could make money. This was the primer of Uncle Sam, who was to me the incarnation of progress, civilization, and freedom.

My adolescent idols were the technicolor images of movie stars. David Niven in his Rolls Royce, driven by a black chauffeur from Harlem. Elizabeth Taylor as the queen of Egypt, worshipped by thousands of Oriental slaves. Gary Cooper leveling his unerring rifle at the head of some Mexican bandit. John Wayne carrying victory over death around the world. They were the invincible whites, superhuman and superb, every man capable of winning a blonde goddess for his love.

In every feature of body and mind I sought to resemble Marlon Brando, James Dean, Frank Sinatra, and Glenn Ford. I wished to be nothing like the bandits whom they killed, the enemies they conquered, the servants who catered to them on the screen. I tried to identify with my heroes and their glory, their wealth, and their power over women. But most of my illusions died with the death of Marilyn Monroe, and a good thing too.

In the city I learned the law of the jungle and the use of intelligence to accumulate riches. I too could learn to be insensitive to other people's sufferings.

Women were brought up to believe in even worse illusions than ours. You were trained to be man's living tools. You were taught to be beautiful. You were taught to walk, smile, sit, bat your eyes, speak, eat, diet, and dress so as to arouse men's desire. You were taught that men are the ones who study, make decisions, build things, make mistakes, give orders, and fulfill themselves. Man is the warrior, woman the warrior's rest. You were to satisfy his whims; to be beautiful, docile, and patient. You must belong to him alone, even if he amused himself with other women. All you had to be was beautiful. It didn't matter if your head had nothing to recommend it but hair. You were the body; he was the mind. He thought; you did. His body was not supposed to matter to you, only his money, his social prestige, his intelligence. That is what you were to look for in him, even though he saw neither your mind nor your spirit, only your body.

The worst poison in our society is not sold at the drug store. It is sex. It is an effect, not a cause. It is the fruit of our inability to love, a symptom of contemporary man's asexuality. We are preoccupied with sex because we are impotent. All the supermen of our childhood were asexual beings. All the movie stars of our adolescence were romantic fakes: They could kiss beautifully, but love was only supposed to happen *after* "The End" flashed on the screen.

In this school we were taught the artifices and the vicissitudes of love, but we never learned to love. A line was drawn between mind and body. As mind, the male has lost his virility, his ability to perceive his body; his sexual aggressiveness stems from the repugnance he feels for his own body. As body, the female has lost her personality, her inner self; her sexual passivity is that of a mere receptacle.

The Don Juans of our day are not supermen, as James Bond might suggest. They are impotent, never-satisfied creatures who must always be trying someone new. And the super-seductress in reality is super-frigid. The body cannot satisfy the mind, and the mind is unaware that it must satisfy the body's spirit.

If you walk in the rain, you are bound to get wet. If we have deceived ourselves about love, then our lives will be ones of amorous deceit and deceptive loves. Only when we discover the social dimension will we free ourselves from this modern Babylon!

(. . .) Only then will we recover the unity of body and mind, of flesh and spirit. Competition will be succeeded by cooperation. Personal success will come to mean success in and for society. Heroism will be the prerogative of the whole people, achieved in the fulfillment of common aspirations. Power will mean service, love, self-giving.

(. . .) Why all these years of psychotherapy? Why all these incurable guilt complexes? They are the price of the illusions in

202

which we have grown up, of the daydreams to which we were addicted. We are maladjusted to life.

At this point it seems to me that the only cure for the evil is to uproot it. But first we must find the roots.

Next time tell me about your daughter. Much friendship to you and your family.

1972

119

To his cousin Agnese

March 27

(. . .) Today I wrote to Father De Couesnongle asking him to forward an appeal to the monasteries that are keeping in touch with our cases. I would like them to help the prisoners' families living in their vicinities. Such a gesture would signify support for us. Only an inmate can appreciate the suffering of a father who knows that his children want food and clothing and are totally dependent on charity. During the past two years we've tried in every way and through various people to organize a permanent relief organization for the families of political prisoners. But our efforts have not succeeded. More than one bishop who has visited us and even the apostolic nuncio promised to set aside a special fund for this purpose and to get help from Caritas International. But nothing concrete has been accomplished, and what aid there is, is intermittent and insufficient.

We have tried to collect a little money for these people by doing all sorts of handicrafts. We have made plastic bags, belts, and leather cigarette cases for the families of poor prisoners to sell. But the market is small, and the prices must be lower than what the stores charge. At least we may have helped a little bit.

Families of political prisoners face far more serious difficulties than families of ordinary offenders. They are the object of general mistrust. The systematic propaganda of the military dictatorship labels us "terrorists" and has managed to panic many people. They are not so much afraid of us as of the police repression that envelops our circle of friends and relations. The wife of a political prisoner loses her job because her boss doesn't want "trouble with the police." His children have trouble finding a school that will accept them, the house is under constant surveillance, and friends gradually fade away. If the family gets any help, the police assume that it comes from some political party or from "the organization" and that it is part of the take from a bank robbery. In some ways the fear and insecurity that the family suffers are worse than what the imprisoned husband must bear.

(. . .) And this is only a small part of the prevailing atmosphere in Brazil today. (. . .) On the surface everything seems just fine. Economic progress is spectacular, and the government supposedly enjoys popular support. This is the image of Great Brazil that they try to project both at home and abroad in order to attract foreign credit and investment. But the reality is very different and has never been as bad as it is today. The lie is well told, however, even as it was in Nazi Germany. The people will end by believing it, just as the Germans believed that Hitler was the savior of Europe.

(. . .) The facts about the situation in Brazil are told in the official publications of the dictatorship, even though official propaganda tries to twist these facts into a favorable interpretation. Just don't believe anyone who comes to Europe to tell you that here everything is fine. German families calmly contemplated the smoke rising from Nazi Germany's "factory" chimneys. When the war was over, they learned that the chimneys belonged to crematoria where human beings were burned to ashes.

A small segment of the church has reacted to the present state of affairs in Brazil. Pedro Casaldaliga, the bishop of São Felix di Araguaia, is our voice crying in the wilderness, our "wilderness" being the *sertão* of Mato Grosso. He courageously defends the small farmers of that region against the huge agribusiness companies that are trying to take away their land at gunpoint. The superintendent of police ordered Lulu, the small farmers' leader, to appear at headquarters for interrogation, and soldiers went to arrest him and escorted him in handcuffs through the streets. The bishop, too, was summoned. But he replied publicly that he was no different from Lulu and that he would wait for the soldiers to arrest him and escort him through the streets in handcuffs. Don't you think that Christ would have done the same?

Repression against the church continues. Last week Father Comblin was expelled from the country. There was no word of it in the press.

Pray for those who wait hopefully to see this sorrowful passion transformed into a glorious resurrection. I want to thank you and your companions for all you have done for us. Hug them all for me, your friend and cousin.

120

To a brother in Rome[75]

Presidente Wenceslau Prison
June 12

(. . .) I am writing to you on the morning of the fourth day of a total fast. It's a magnificent, sunny day that seems to reflect our own feelings.

(. . .) We are reviving an age-old tradition that of late has fallen into oblivion. Fasting fortifies the spirit. It is as if we are living Christ's words: "The flesh is weak but the spirit gives life." The atmosphere is one of spiritual retreat. We pray continually and nourish ourselves on God's word. It is a kind of Exodus. We are crossing a desert with only manna for food, accompanied by the certainty that we will attain the liberation of the Brazilian people. This certainty is grounded in our faith in Christ the Redeemer, and in our loving communion with the people. We choose to be present among the people and to walk with them through this parched and seemingly endless desert, bearing in our hearts the certainty of liberation. We are not downhearted and we never have been. We are happy because the Lord is with us and the church of God is here in our two-by-five-meter cell. . . .

June 30

(. . .) To prevent any misunderstandings, I will try to give you a detailed and faithful account of recent events.

At the beginning of May we learned that fifteen political prisoners would be taken from Tiradentes Prison and isolated from their companions. They would be the first group. The aim of the military was to gradually weed out the "incorrigibles" from those who could be "rehabilitated," naturally according to the military's definition of these terms. We were in immediate danger of maltreatment and even murder, presumably incurred while "attempting escape" or "attempting revolt" or "during brawls with other prisoners." There have been nasty precedents for this happening in other places. An enormous number of political prisoners have "disappeared" while "resisting the police." In reality they died as a result of terrible torture or were murdered in cold blood after unspeakable suffering. The method is much used today by the political police all over Brazil.

In the face of this imminent great danger, our lawyers lodged all sorts of protests. They were summoned, questioned, and exhaustively investigated by the political police. Petitions were sent to newspapers, journals, and prominent people. All in vain. Only one defense was left to us: to stay together in the prison for political prisoners. We had to adopt a common position that corresponded to the gravity of our situation.

On May 12 eighteen of us were taken out of Tiradentes Prison and transferred to the state penitentiary, where we were to be treated like ordinary offenders. (. . .) Once we got there, we were put in cells with the most dangerous criminals. We then began our fast, declaring that we would not touch food until we were returned to our companions. Those who had remained at Tiradentes Prison joined in a sympathy fast. Our archbishop, who fully grasped the situation, agreed to serve as our negotiator with the authorities. He did everything he could to meet with the participants in this gesture of denunciation and protest, but humiliating obstacles were put in his way. Meanwhile our friends in Tiradentes who were fasting in sympathy were transferred to the São Paulo House of Detention.

On the sixth day of our fast, a member of the São Paulo judiciary came to us, stating that he had carte blanche to resolve the situation. He promised us that if we stopped our fast, within a week all political prisoners would be reunited in one cell bloc in the House of Detention, and that women prisoners would be taken to a nearby prison so that their relatives could visit them again. On the basis of this formal commitment from the authorities we broke our fast, and two days later we too were transferred to the House of Detention. But as time went on, we realized that we had been shamefully deceived. Only those who had gone on a hunger strike out of sympathy with us would remain in the House of Detention. We and other "dangerous" prisoners would be kept in isolation. Our situation had not changed; indeed it had become even more perilous. We repeatedly asked to see the official who had made the promise to us, but without success. But we did get to explain our plight to Archbishop Arns of São Paulo, and he did succeed in getting to see us.

On June 8, without notice, we were awakened at 4:00 A.M. to "take a trip." There were six of us: three Dominicans, a lawyer who had been arrested with Mother Maurina, a godson of Monsignor Alano du Noday, and a student. The judge made some veiled threats, but we were not told where they intended to take us. The guards were from DOPS, the political police unit that has tortured and killed countless people. Among them are some members of the death squad in São Paulo. We were pushed into a windowless police van, and in airless darkness and suffocating heat we traveled all day without food or water. Fernando fainted, the student had a violent attack of dysentery, and the lawyer, who had been tortured, suffered racking back pain. At 9:00 P.M. we arrived at our destination and found ourselves at Presidente Wenceslau Penitentiary on the border between Mato Grosso and São Paulo, 660 kilometers from where we had started.

Faced with this new official lawlessness, we again took up our fast. It was the only means of defense available to us. (. . .) We began on June 9, so we are now on the twenty-second day. (. . .)

Of our companions back in São Paulo we have heard relatively little. They are all in isolation. On June 9 two of them, Paulo de Tarso Vanuchi and Paulo de Tarso Wenceslau, were carted off to the headquarters of *Operação Bandeirantes* and brutally tortured for five days in an attempt to get them to stop their fast. Right now they are in São Paulo prison hospital, in what condition we do not know. (. . .) For a week we have been subjected to real psychological tortures by the doctor assigned to "take care" of us. . . . Bishop José Gonçalves of Presidente Prudente has been of great help and comfort to us. He has done everything possible—and some things impossible—to help us. Without him I do not know what might have become of us.

That's what has happened to us in the last month. We do not know how long this situation will go on. We only know that our fellowship with other political prisoners—present and future—is the Christian witness that we are called upon to bear. Nothing compels us to this course except the love of Jesus Christ, who chose to give his life for humanity's salvation. One figure is constantly in our minds' eyes: Blessed Maximilian Kolbe. If he could lay down his life for one laborer, then we feel that risking ours to save thousands—workers, farmers, students, intellectuals, religious, and priests—is truly meaningful in God's plan.

We were not surprised to have lost our appeal to the Supreme Tribunal. It was just another attempt. But that tribunal, like all the others in Brazil, is mostly composed of and dominated by military men who have inflicted an unlawful government on us and have turned torture and political assassination into our bitter daily bread.

We are determined to continue our fast as part of the Christian witness we must offer at this terrible moment in the history of our country and the Brazilian church. It must continue at least until we have news of our companions in São Paulo. In this connection the return of our archbishop to Brazil is most important, for he continues to be our negotiator.

I hope I have clarified everything. We count on your support.

July 28

(. . .) Our situation today is not what it was when I wrote my last letter to you. We were then in the infirmary, in the course of a total fast that lasted thirty-three days. (. . .) When we finally ended the fast, we went through days of tense waiting. Would we be kept here? Would we be returned to São Paulo? (. . .) Finally we learned our fate: We will be kept here like common prisoners. (. . .) On the twenty-fifth we were processed into the population of this prison. This means that we are now known by numbers: Betto 25044, Fernando 25045, Ivo 25046, Vanderley Caixa 25047, Maurice Politi 25048, Manoel Porfirio de Souza 25049. We wear the prison uniform, we are not allowed food parcels from home, and we must follow prison regulations. Since they were made for a population of four hundred inmates, they are hardly flexible enough to allow for individual needs.

We are also subject to the same punishments as the other prisoners. These range from a simple warning through loss of visiting rights to solitary confinement. We live in individual cells, two meters by three, one next to the other. In each cell is a toilet, cement blocks that serve as chair and table, and a faucet for washing our dishes and ourselves. In the afternoon we can be together in one room; there we study theology.

(. . .) The other prisoners' attitudes toward us are excellent. They all come to talk and listen to us. They show us great sympathy and seem immensely curious on the subject of faith. We feel useful. (. . .) We protest the regimen to which we have been subjected, but we find ourselves adapting to it bit by bit. It is the radicalism of the gospel that bids us to do so. Now we must share our lives wholly with our brothers, the ordinary offenders, and carry on our struggle for the justice to which we are entitled. As always, we are counting on your prayers.

121

To his cousin Agnese

Presidente Wenceslau Prison Infirmary
July 15

I am rereading your letter of June 4, which came together with a most beautiful postcard. Receiving it amid these tribulations was like sighting a port of hope in a storm. You simply cannot imagine what these last three months have been like for us. In the granaries of the Lord the seed is winnowed for a long time. . . . Is it so that it will bear more fruit?

On May 12 Fernando, Ivo, and I—with fifteen fellow prisoners—were taken from Tiradentes, which housed the political prisoners of São Paulo, and transported to the state penitentiary, where the ordinary offenders are kept. For the first time since we had been deprived of our physical liberty, we were obliged to wear prison uniforms, to be clean-shaven, and to inhabit individual cells, and were forbidden to receive mail from friends or relatives. Even religious assistance was denied us, and Archbishop Arns of São Paulo was forbidden to visit us.

For these reasons, and also with a view to returning to Tiradentes where political prisoners are held, we began a total fast, taking only water. After a week we were again transferred, this time to the House of Detention in São Paulo, which houses five thousand ordinary prisoners. But we had been promised that all the political prisoners would be reunited there in a cell block of their own. We stopped our fast and got some improvement in our condition: We still had to wear uniforms, but we were allowed visitors.

About three weeks went by and the promised reunification of all political prisoners did not take place. On June 8, toward evening, the colonel in charge of the House of Detention informed us that early the next day we three Dominicans and three other political prisoners would be transferred again, but he did not say where. We traveled 660 kilometers, handcuffed to each other in an enclosed truck without light or air, which the burning sun turned into an oven. Toward evening of that day we arrived, more dead than alive, in the town of Presidente Wenceslau, on the border between São Paulo and Mato Grosso. We are now interned in this regional prison, which presently holds about four hundred ordinary prisoners.

On June 9 the six of us who were transferred here and the other twenty-six political prisoners remaining in the House of Detention began to fast once again. We fasted until July 11—thirty-three days in all. Try to imagine what it was like to go all that time without food, stretched on a bed, being fed intravenously. The catabolism induced by undernourishment consumed our fat and our muscles, causing infections in some of us and various manifestations of hyperacidity in others. Our nervous systems were abraded by isolation and by the effort of resisting those who tried to get us to eat. I kept thinking about the martyrdom of Eleazar, in chapter 6 of the second book of Maccabees.

Finally, on July 10, our fellow prisoners in São Paulo broke their fast and asked us to do the same while waiting for a response from the authorities. We heard about it on July 11, but it was not until yesterday (July 14) that we were able to take solid food. That's how weak we had become.

In all this, however, I feel that God's grace is lending strength to our weakness, that our inner selves are maturing and developing. I am content to think that this sacrifice may, in a more evangelical church that "does justice," turn into a boon.

I thank you for your words of encouragement, and for the love of all of you who pray for us and think about us. You are ever present in my prayers. A big hug and much friendship to you all. May Our Lady of Liberation bless us.

122

To the Dominican Provincial Chapter

September 6

Since circumstances prevent us from attending the upcoming Provincial Chapter in Belo Horizonte, we are sending you this letter in response to your request. It is a modest summary of what our lives as Dominicans have been during these three years in prison.

For us prison has become a privileged locale of Christian living. Although we did not choose prison, it has all the same forced upon us a transformation that would have been very difficult to accomplish on the outside. Suffering, viewed in the context of the cross, cannot but be purifying and liberating.

The very fact of being arrested tore us away from the essentially bourgeois world in which we had been living. Accidental and superfluous things ceased to be regarded as fundamental and indispensable. In our fellow inmates our apostolic vocation found a very specific focus, freeing us from the vacillation of continual searching for a genuine field of missionary endeavor. . . .

Prison has defined a mission territory for us, and in a way it has forced us to take it seriously. . . . Prison has imposed on us the great responsibility of being the only church presence within various prisons. . . . We have come to realize that it is impossible to know people unless you live with them. Our living with other prisoners has afforded some of them a chance to rediscover the church, to see the advent of a church without privileges. Yet we know we are still very far from being as poor as they. We have many friends and brothers in the faith who are interested in what is happening to us, whereas most prisoners spend five, ten, even fifteen years in prison without one visitor!

Among our fellow inmates, we try continually to stress the Christian and ecclesial character of our life. We have been doing this since our first days in prison. . . . Even though most of the prisoners are not Christian, yet in a way they expect and implicitly demand that we live as men of faith here in prison. They marvel at our attitudes, which might seem very traditional, and they lose confidence when they see something in us that contradicts their image of a Christian.

We practice common prayer and meditation on the gospel. Our prison companions would not understand living among Christians who did not pray. We commemorate, simply but meaningfully, all the important feasts of the liturgical year. And in their fashion our fellow inmates have always participated.

We have often asked ourselves what it means to be Dominicans in prison. In practice, very little. Perhaps a certain type of Christian education marked by respect for theological reflection. What's important here is not the label attached to our way of being Christians but just our way of being Christians. Thus it doesn't matter whether one is a secular priest or a Jesuit or a Franciscan. Here reality imposes on everyone the same pattern of life and the same tasks and forces us to form a single community. Only rich people can distinguish between one congregation and religious order and another. To the poor we all are priests and Christians, and what matters is how we act.

Although we are outside the framework of monastic life, we have never before lived such a deeply communitarian and regular life. Here there is no room for theory divorced from practice. We are among prisoners and guards twenty-four hours a day, and this imposes upon us consistency and integrity. We cannot be one person in public and another in private. We must put up with everything: For us there is no "getting away from it all" to the company of close friends, or to a movie, or on a vacation. We cannot even choose our friends. Prison brings together very different people—there is no way of avoiding each other. Prison discipline imposes on us a life of strict observance.

In actual fact the little Christian community we form amid our fellow prisoners represents a communion with them. Despite the limitations imposed on us by prison, we try to provide a basis for our thinking and to continue our study of philosophy and theology. To answer our fellow prisoners' challenge—which is also the challenge now facing the church—we must pay attention to philosophy, economics, and sociology. These disciplines have afforded us a more scientific picture not only of human relations but of just how it is that *people make history.* The fact that we are, of necessity and by the very nature of our discussions, self-taught has allowed us to discover which theological problems rank highest among the concerns of God's people. This is one of the most interesting aspects of our life in prison.

Sharing the same life as the other prisoners has given us a better understanding of what it means to be leaven in the dough. Personal problems of a psychological and subjective nature disappear when we devote ourselves to other people's problems. Here we are continually called upon for something; we are laden with present tasks.

We have never allowed discord among us. So far this unity has certainly been one of the most important aspects of our witness. Many fellow inmates express their regret at not being able to achieve a similar unity among themselves. We also refuse to accept privileges without, however, ceasing to fight for our rights. In every situation we make a deliberate effort to think and act with the full realization that we are the presence of the church in prison. . . .

We are convinced that in the wake of Vatican II God's Spirit has initiated a new *metanoia,* a process of conversion, in God's people and in human history. We believe that this time the renewal of the church will not be effected by isolated individuals like Dominic and Francis but will grow out of the evangelical life of the Christian community as it learns to follow the Lord along the path of poverty and persecution (see Luke 8). Our experience among these people has provided us with some building blocks toward a people's pastorship.

There are many difficulties, some of them insurmountable. The prison officials will not let us do apostolic work or even administer the sacraments. But is it not more important that we Christians ourselves become the Lord's sacrament among the people?

Such has been the nature of our presence in prison so far.

There is no merit in what we are doing because there is nothing else we can do. Either you try to live what you preach or you become a prisoner of your own charade. Affectionate greetings to you all.

123

To his cousin

I got your letter of November 1 last Friday. I'm surprised that you haven't received mine, the one in which I commented on your meetings in Sotto il Monte regarding Christian praxis and prayer. In that letter I also spoke of the meaning that we are trying to give to our presence here among the ordinary prisoners and I pointed out the vast difference between a church that does good works for the poor and a church that is in communion with the poor. I said that unfortunately we are used to *going to* the poor with armloads of gifts, but it would be better if our arms were empty so that we could embrace the poor and shake their hands. I reminded you that now is the time for the church to *align itself with* the disinherited and the oppressed, as Peter and John did with the cripple outside the temple: "I have no silver or gold; but what I have I give you: in the name of Jesus Christ of Nazareth, walk" (Acts 3:5–6). I also asked you to send me the book by that young monk who spoke to you on the subject of prayer. That was the gist of my letter that was apparently lost.

Here in Brazil it's often said that Vatican II has made no difference at all in Europe, but from your letter I gather that this is not generally true and that there are people and groups intensely engaged in the process of return to the gospel. I am convinced that authentic renewal will come, with us or without us. The Holy Spirit does not ask permission to act. Those who have ears to hear will hear, those who have eyes to see will see.

Early every morning, before the cart with the carafes of

coffee comes around, I meditate on the gospels. Today, reading Matthew 27:33–50, I was struck by the atmosphere of failure surrounding Jesus' agony. It is easy to follow him through the triumphal entry into Jerusalem, but there is a real temptation to abandon him when the persecution begins. Jesus could have confounded his persecutors by coming down from the cross and proving he was the Son of God, but he did not give in to triumphalism and would not use any means not in accord with the will of his Father. At times I feel that the church has never learned to tolerate disdain and derision, that it preens itself in the mirror of worldly wisdom. We are afraid to experience the dynamics of failure. We are afraid that the cross will turn out to be a real cross that lacerates our body and spirit. We prefer to remain safe and secure inside the city walls.

In contrast to Jesus, we want to prove to the powerful of this world that we are the children of God. We do not wish to be confused with those whom the world rejects. . . .

I think the subject of your meeting in Sotto il Monte was well chosen. Praxis is a very serious problem for Christians today. We live in a world whose political and juridical principles —which we accept—do not correspond to its existing social relationships. Religion is in the same boat to the extent that we fail to live the faith we profess.

Our social relationships are profoundly characterized by individualism. It isn't easy to preach love in a situation where competition and getting the better of others seem to be the only road to professional success. Hence it is of fundamental importance for us to create fellowship with those who possess nothing except the power to make all people free and equal. This is the fertile soil in which we must plant the seed of God's word, the seed that fructifies the world.

Our lawyer has requested that we be released on bail, and the Military Council will make its decision next month. We are prepared to spend another year in prison. It would be a real surprise to get out any sooner. What others regard as privation is gain for us. (. . .)

1973

124

To his cousin Agnese

January 2

This is in reply to the letter you wrote me exactly a month ago on the First Sunday of Advent. So far I haven't been able to find out whether you got my other letters. I have answered all of yours, but I have no idea whether you got mine because you make no reference to them. Besides I don't have your new address, so I can't write to you directly.

You say that in Italy a lot of people are asking: "What do you believe in now?" You also talk about the need for finding new sources of spirituality. It is precisely this need, I think, that makes it possible to answer such a question.

The problem is a consequence of theology's growing maturity expressed in its ability to criticize its own premises. Nowadays there is nothing that cannot be questioned. Just as in the latter half of the nineteenth century, post-Hegelian philosophy criticized the methodology and the objectives of everything that had come before, so today theology is impelled to a similarly radical self-revision. Among Catholics this process began with Vatican II and constitutes a real Copernican revolution. Just consider the problems raised by Bultmann, for example. . . .

Scientific progress is the root of all philosophical progress. One cannot write a history of philosophy without taking into account the data arising from man's perception of nature. Plato was the genius beneficiary of Greek mathematics, as Descartes was of Galileo's physics, Kant of Newton's discoveries, and Marx of the English economists.

Theology is not an isolated science. It cannot help but reflect innovations in science and philosophy. But theology has had a falling-out with the secular sciences. Science has definitely become the mainspring of all human progress. Philosophy has ceased to contemplate the world and has decided to change it. But what about theology? Will it manage to be more than a polite way of saying something about revealed truths?

"What do you believe in now?" People find the question

223

hard to answer and the reason for the difficulty, I think, is the centuries-long divorce between theology and spirituality in the Western church. You say, quite rightly, that we must discover new sources of spirituality. I think we can only accomplish this through a new mode of theologizing in which theology and spirituality will be inextricably linked. The foundation of theology nowadays is threefold: divine revelation, tradition, and signs of the times. Theological interpretation of the signs of the times is not something new; the Old Testament prophets did it long ago. It is new only for us who have reinstituted it after long disuse, albeit we still lack the tools to practice it. We must clean our glasses well to see what's happening in the world. Otherwise we will be in danger of mistaking the burning bush, the breeze on Mount Horeb, and the star over Bethlehem for purely natural phenomena.

Every historical period has its own structures. To understand the period we must know how these structures were formed, for the word of God is supposed to reverberate through them. Hence a contemporary theologian simply must know how to judge the impact of economics as a determining element in the lives of peoples and in international relations. It is not enough to say *what* we must do to be faithful to the Lord. One must also spell out *how* we are to do it, what our praxis should be, how we must act within the context of our fidelity to him. Chapter 21 of Luke's gospel presents a masterful lesson by Jesus on reading and interpreting the signs of the times. He tells us the sign: Jerusalem besieged by an invading army. He tells us the outcome: Its destruction is at hand. Then he tells people how to act according to their circumstances: Those in Judea are to flee to the mountains; those in Jerusalem are to get away. Those in the countryside are not to enter the city. Then he reveals the meaning of the event: These are days of chastisement in which all that had been written will be fulfilled.

The church finds it hard to interpret present-day events prophetically. It seems perplexed by events like the war in Vietnam, the struggle in the Middle East, the various wars of liberation, the emancipation of women, student and worker movements, dictatorships. . . . In general the hierarchy limits itself to voicing vague desires for peace without giving any concrete indications of how committed Christians should act in these real situations. Hence it's hard for the church to show the profound significance of Christian praxis for the course of salvation.

I believe that two ideological factors influence the positions that the hierarchy takes. First of all, prophecy has given way to diplomatic expediency. Pronouncements are phrased so as to offend no one, therefore they touch no one. They provoke no questioning, no changes of heart. The second factor is the false notion that the world can evolve without birth pangs. This fallacy is reflected in the pessimistic attitude toward all social conflicts, as if they represented a backward step. But Jesus tells us exactly the opposite: "When you hear of wars and insurrections, do not fall into a panic. These things are bound to happen first; but the end does not follow immediately. . . . When all this begins to happen, *stand upright and hold your heads high, because your liberation is near*" (Luke 21:9–28).

I can see the possibility of a synthesis between theology and spirituality only in an evangelical praxis. We ask each other, What do you believe in now? because the object of our faith is a body of doctrines subjected to rigorous criticism. That sort of faith should not exist among us. The true object of a Christian's faith is a person, Jesus Christ; and the relationship established by faith is one of love. Whoever experiences a crisis of faith because the assumptions of theology are being revised confesses thereby that he lacks spirituality. By spirituality I mean a way of possessing Christ in one's own life, not merely as someone believed in but above all as someone loved. Theology must be rooted in love.

When we observe Jesus' relations with his apostles, we are amazed to find that he was never concerned to transmit to them a body of doctrine. He did not copy the Greek Academy or even the Hebrew synagogue. He did not train his disciples in the manner of Plato and Aristotle. We do not find in the gospel an academic Jesus, concerned to demonstrate to his disciples the principles in which they are to believe. In Christianity the object of faith is a person, which implies a relationship of love.

225

Jesus is one who loves and who is loved. He lives with his friends and teaches them what the simplest happenings of life mean in the light of the "good news." He is not in a hurry, and their vacillation does not upset him. Peter vacillates. So does Thomas. And Matthew tells us that some were unsure even after they had seen him risen from the dead (Matt. 28:17). But they all loved him.

So the question should be phrased differently: "What do you love? A person may believe everything that the church tells him to believe, and still love worldly wisdom, the trappings of luxury, money, and power. When a person tells you what he loves, he reveals who he really is: "For where your treasure is, there will your heart be also" (Matt. 6:21). Belief without love is possible only when theology and spirituality are completely separated. We have much to learn from the Eastern church about how to overcome this defect. The Eastern church has no such dualism. Its theology is not *rational science* but *wisdom*, and it grows out of and is nurtured by a profoundly spiritual life.

Latin rationalism has so subdivided the duties of Christians that we have ended by losing the unity and dynamism of the gospel. Some are to contemplate; others to act. Some are to be concerned for the poor, others not. Some are to follow the beatitudes, others may even observe the evangelical counsels.

This is a serious distortion. I don't think that Jesus established different categories of Christians. The so-called evangelical counsels are for all: priests and laypeople, married people and celibates. So are prayer and contemplation.

The only allowable differences are in charisms and functions. All the other differences derive from our imperfections and our infidelity.

Well, I'll sign off. At home everything is fine. Mom and Dad have celebrated their thirty-first wedding anniversary, and Leonardo has gone to the United States. Please let me know whether you've gotten this letter. Keep writing to me. Fernando, Ivo, and I send you and your friends all our best wishes for a happy 1973.

226

A Prisoner's Prayer

Lord,
when you look down on those who have imprisoned us and given
us over to torture,
when you weigh the actions of our jailers and the heavy
sentences imposed on us,
when you pass judgment on the lives of those who have
humiliated us
and on the consciences of those who have cast us aside,
forget, Lord, the evil they may have done.
Remember instead that through this sacrifice
we have been brought closer to your crucified son:
Through torture we have received the imprint of his wounds;
through these bars, the freedom of his spirit;
through our sentences, the hope of his kingdom
and the joy of being his sons through humiliation.
Remember, Lord,
that this suffering has borne fruit in us,
like the winnowed seed sprouting.
It is the fruit of justice and peace,
of light and love.

Epilogue

Betto was released from prison in October 1973, and today lives in a shanty in a desperately poor section of Vitória, capital of the state of Espírito Santo. Together with other young people, he is participating in the life of the poor to concretize his commitment to the oppressed. According to him it is not a matter of trying to serve them but above all to be one of them. Betto believes only in a church that is born of the people.

One year after his release from prison he said: "We have finished the first year in freedom and we have not found freedom; it still does not exist. I try always to be prepared, knowing the next time will be the last." (Betto is referring to a new imprisonment.)

With regard to his status in the Dominican order, Betto has written to his general superior asking that he be officially considered a lay brother: "I do not want to be ordained a priest because it would be the first step in rising to power within the church. I am more convinced every day that any type of power tends to corrupt. Furthermore, the priority is no longer sacramental but rather evangelical and I can continue to evangelize without being ordained a priest."

Notes

Foreword

1. All abbreviations are explained on page xiii.

2. Later, in 1969, when the military dictatorship had gained firm control, Bishop Padim felt compelled to point out and denounce the Nazi matrix of the doctrine of "development" as propagated by the War College of the Brazilian generals.

3. Insofar as prison witness is concerned, Christian resistance to fascism was elaborated doctrinally by Emmanuel Mounier and Dietrich Bonhoeffer. Mounier, a Catholic philosopher, was prosecuted and imprisoned by the Vichy government in 1942. Bonhoeffer, a Protestant theologian and minister, was hanged in 1944 by the Nazis in the Flossenburg concentration camp. This thinking found its most forceful embodiment in the German Evangelical community known as the "Confessing Church," whose leader and inspiration was the Berlin minister, Martin Niemöller. It was Niemöller who raised the cry of resistance against Nazism. During Hitler's rule, eighteen of these "Confessing" ministers were shot and several hundred were imprisoned. Niemöller himself was imprisoned for eight years.

1969

4. "If the world hates you, it hated me first, as you know well. If you belonged to the world, the world would love its own; but because you do not belong to the world, because I have chosen you out of the world, for that reason the world hates you. Remember what I said: 'A servant is not greater than his master.' As they persecuted me, they will persecute you; they will follow your teaching as little as they have followed mine. It is on my account that they will treat you thus, because they do not know the One who sent me. . . . I have told you all this to guard you against the breakdown of your faith. They will ban you from the synagogue; indeed, the time is coming when anyone who kills you will suppose that he is performing a religious duty. They will do these things because they do not know either the Father or me. I have told you all this so that when the time comes for it to happen, you may remember my warning."

5. Tiradentes is an old prison in downtown São Paulo, built in the colonial

era. Abandoned for decades because of its unhygienic conditions, it has recently been returned to use, primarily for political prisoners.

6. A secondary school run by the Barnabite Fathers in Belo Horizonte, where Betto studied.

7. Teresa is Betto's sister. She moved to São Paulo to be near him in prison.

1970

8. All subsequent letters are written from Tiradentes Prison in São Paulo unless otherwise noted.

9. "Acts" are official pronouncements and decrees. Here Betto is referring specifically to presidential proclamations which suspend constitutional guarantees and promulgate extraordinary measures.

10. Café Filho was president of Brazil during the transition period between the violent death of Getulio Vargas and the electoral victory of Juscelino Kubitschek (1956–1961).

11. Pinto is an outstanding lawyer, still living, who has served as attorney for the defense in many political trials under various dictatorships.

12. The son of Luiz Fernando, Betto's older brother to whom this letter is addressed.

13. Dom Pedro I (1798–1834) was the son of the Portuguese ruler, Dom João VI, who fled to Brazil as Napoleon's army approached his country. Pedro grew up in Brazil. On September 7, 1822, on the banks of the Ipiranga River in São Paulo, he proclaimed Brazil's independence from Portugal. His proclamation is known as the *Grito do Ipiranga*.

14. A division of the political security police in São Paulo.

15. Betto is referring to another Dominican, Tito de Alencar. He was one of the seventy political prisoners released in exchange for the Swiss ambassador in December 1970.

16. In this torture the victim is trussed to a bar and swung back and forth. Electrodes and other torture devices may be used on him.

17. *Caritas Internationalis* is the Holy See's equivalent of the Red Cross.

18. The New State was the fascist regime inaugurated by Getulio Vargas in 1937.

19. Felinto Muller was the infamous chief of the political security police under Getulio Vargas.

20. Taubate is a small city in the state of São Paulo.

21. Betto's youngest brother.

22. Betto shared a cell with "nonpolitical prisoners," that is, ordinary offenders.

23. "Leo" is Betto's second youngest brother, Leonardo.

24. A national daily of conservative bent, now the official voice of the regime.

25. Kidnapped by antigovernment guerrillas, the Japanese consul was released in exchange for five political prisoners.

26. Mother Maurina Borges was the mother superior of an orphanage in Ribeirão Preto. She was arrested for giving refuge to members of a resistance group. When it became known that she had been tortured, the bishop of

Ribeirão Preto excommunicated the local chief of police. She is presently in exile in Mexico.

27. Demetrius was the silversmith of Ephesus who incited a riot against St. Paul because he feared Paul's preaching would put an end to his livelihood (see Acts 19).

28. Pedro is a member of a religious order and a biblical exegete.

29. The "Dominican Affair" was the name given by the secret police to their campaign against the Dominican order.

30. Antonio Carlos, the youngest child in the family.

31. Seminary in the city of São Leopoldo, in the state of Rio Grande do Sul, where Betto was studying at the time of his arrest.

32. Giorgio Callegari, an Italian Dominican. Betto refers to him as Giorgio or Father Giorgio.

33. Tiradentes (1748–92), a Brazilian patriot whose real name was José Joaquim da Silva Xavier. He led a revolutionary movement against Portuguese rule and was eventually executed in Rio de Janeiro.

34. Pedro Alvares Cabral (ca. 1467–ca. 1520), a Portuguese navigator, discovered the coast of Brazil in 1500.

35. Gerardo de Proença Sigaud, Archbishop of Diamantina, and two or three other bishops constitute a faction of the Brazilian episcopacy that is aggressively opposed to church renewal. Founder of the TFP movement (Tradition, Family, Property), he is a friend and advisor of the military government.

36. From this point on Betto is speaking to his sister Cecilia and her husband, though the letter is addressed only to his parents.

37. A club in Belo Horizonte much frequented by playboys.

38. From 1960 to 1964, students active in the Belo Horizonte JEC used to meet for Mass every day at 6:00 P.M. in a downtown church. This daily mass became so well-known a meeting-place and so significant for the development of a theology of history that is was prohibited and its participants persecuted after the coup of March 31, 1964. Among the students this Mass was known as the "six o'clock tea."

39. State in the central Brazilian plateau, where the present capital (Brasilia) is located.

40. A reference to Rolf Hochhuth's play of the same name about Pius XII.

41. Onganía was president of Argentina from 1966 to 1970.

42. The case dealt with the clandestine activities of the UNE, which had been officially disbanded in 1964. Nearly all of its members were ambushed by the police and arrested in October 1968 during their clandestine national convention at a farm near São Paulo.

43. The letter is addressed to one of the many Christian youth groups in São Paulo.

44. Author of classic Brazilian novels in the realistic tradition.

45. A gold mine in Belo Horizonte.

46. Brazilian TV personality.

47. G.A. Vilaça, *O nariz do morto* (Rio de Janeiro: JCN Editora, 1970).

48. Father Domingos Maia Leite is at present the provincial superior of the Dominican order in Brazil.

49. The convent where Sister Marike lives.

50. The bishop of Crateus, a small diocese in northeast Brazil. He is well known for his stand against the large landed estates and in favor of rural unions. On several occasions he has defied the military in order to protect the

rights of the peasants. He divided the property of his diocese into small holdings and gave them to anyone willing to cultivate them.

51. Betto is referring to the kidnapping of the Swiss ambassador, who was later released in exchange for seventy political prisoners.

52. See letter 22 and note 26.

53. Tito de Alencar, released in exchange for the Swiss consul.

54. The reader must remember that when it is winter in the northern hemisphere it is summer in the southern hemisphere.

55. A Brazilian convent of contemplative nuns.

56. The movement of liturgical renewal was introduced into Brazil in about 1940 by Benedictines in a monastery in Rio de Janeiro. It was associated with the movement of Catholic Action at that time.

57. The new archbishop of São Paulo, appointed after Archbishop Rossi was transferred to Rome.

58. Sister Ruth is Betto's cousin and contemporary.

1971

59. In a plenary session (held in Belo Horizonte, February 1971) the Brazilian episcopate sent letters of support and solidarity to the archbishop of São Paulo (Evaristo Arns), the bishop of Volta Redonda (Valdir Calheiros), and the provincial of the Dominican order (Domingos Maia Leite).

60. "The defendant receives the benefit of the doubt."

61. A priest from Milan serving in the Pontifical Foreign Missions.

62. Archbishop Evaristo Arns, O.F.M.

63. The newsletter of the São Paulo Catholic Information Center reported this visit in its May issue. The superior general of the Dominican order (Father Aniceto Fernández) was allowed to visit the Dominican prisoners, and he concelebrated Mass in their cell. Asked for his impressions, he expressed his wonderment at their high spirits. He said the prisoners were not "downhearted, aggressive, or dispirited but rather strong and serene in their priestly and religious vocation, . . . imbued with a strong sense of the Christian import of their presence in prison."

64. Italian missionary in the Congregation of the Servants of Mary. Acre is a "territory" belonging to the Brazilian Federal Republic, located in the far north of the country near the borders of Peru and Bolivia. It differs from the regular Brazilian states in being still partly unexplored borderland and not fully integrated into the juridical, economic, and political structure of the country.

65. The baby is the daughter of Claudia, Betto's cousin.

66. Dr. Gilberto Gomes Libanio, brother of Betto's mother.

67. Archbishop of São Paulo. See letter 102.

68. The missionary mentioned in letter 103.

69. Father Giulio Vicini. See letter 102.

70. The request was rejected in June 1971. See letter 116.

71. Seminarian mentioned in letter 102.

72. Apostolic letter of Paul VI, issued in May 1971 to commemorate the eightieth anniversary of *Rerum Novarum.* An English translation appears in *The Pope Speaks* magazine, Washington, D.C. 16:137–68, and in *The Gospel of Peace*

and Justice: Catholic Social Teaching since Pope John, presented by Joseph Gremillion (Maryknoll, New York: Orbis Books, 1976).

73. General Assembly of the Latin American Bishops held in Medellín, Colombia, in 1968. The full proceedings are available in English translation from the Latin American Division of the United States Catholic Conference in Washington.

74. After serving his sentence and being released from prison, Father Vicini was acquitted on appeal in August 1971.

1972

75. These are excerpts from three different letters, grouped together because they deal with the same subject and are addressed to the same person. These and all subsequent letters were written in Presidente Wenceslau Prison.

Index of Major Themes

Numbers refer to letters in this volume, not to pages.

awareness
   and Christianity, 38, 95
   freedom of, 99
   need for, 28, 68, 95

Bible
   and failures of exegesis, 26, 52, 82
   and praxis, 38, 82, 95, 115
   and the promise to Abraham and Jesus, 28
   misreading of, 95

Bonhoeffer, Dietrich, 23, 26

capitalism, 40, 95

celibacy, 81, 104

chastity, meaning of vow of, 104

Christ
   as our way to God, 70, 79, 115
   as sign of contradiction, 10, 115, 116
   criminals and the poor as the living image of, 23, 76, 88, 90, 119
   death and resurrection of, 23, 29, 96, 108, 119
   following, and the cross, 5, 6, 9, 14, 23, 24, 70, 91, 102, 104, 108, 115, 123,
      124
   Incarnation of, 23, 88
   presence of, in prison, 4, 12, 24
   seeming failure of, 102, 123
   sharing in prison the Christmas mystery of, 10, 12, 86, 90, 92
   social behavior of, 52, 112

Christians and the church
   absent voice of, 54, 95, 124
   and cowardice, 82
   and custom of aiding fugitives, 91
   and failure of church language, 26, 82
   and failure to emphasize praxis, 38, 95, 102, 123

and failures of Vatican II, 26, 68
and ineffective social encyclicals, 58, 112
and their message wrongly identified with status quo, 45, 70, 102
as questioning history, 28
as slow to act, 19, 107
catechesis insensitive to present history of, 95
contemplative life of, 55, 88, 104
depersonalization of, 90
facing radical change, 55, 56, 90, 113
from monasticism to worldly power, 117
increasing courage of in Brazil, 101
in prison, 5, 9, 23, 30, 41, 78, 88, 91, 98, 116, 120, 122
legitimizing wrongdoing, 45, 53, 68, 90, 113
must serve human beings, 104
need for risk of, 28, 44, 88, 95, 112, 123
paternalism of, 40
persecuted, 66
prison as sign of, 9, 14, 19, 28, 30, 96, 116, 120
privatizing faith and morality of, 55, 56, 57, 82, 95, 102, 110
prophetic function of, not exercised, 28, 51, 54, 102, 124
renewal at work in, 30, 55, 68, 81, 115, 123
responsibility of, 81, 95, 104, 112, 116
true nature of, 9, 104
unnecessary structures of, 81
unsound perspectives of, 40
vis-à-vis changing world, 115

commitment, to the dignity of man, 23, 108

community
    learning, in prison, 20, 26, 86, 111, 122,
    of mankind, 66, 78, 96

contemplative life, 67, 70, 75, 88, 104

culture, dangers in values of, 55

development, myth of, 112

East, as more spiritually developed than West, 15, 124

ecumenism, in prison, 26, 117

eschatology, see kingdom of God

Eucharist, meditation on, 12, 110

faith
    and joy, 1, 3
    as distinct from culture, 55
    now divorced from praxis, 117, 124
    solidified by prison, 97, 99, 116, 121

fascism, 18, 103

fast, as protest, 120, 121

freedom
    as the last great discovery of humankind, 25, 96, 124

definition of, 23, 25, 64, 97, 106
as illusory in West, 15, 25
inner, 5, 6, 7, 24, 25, 28, 47, 72, 97, 113
yearning for, in prison, 83, 92

Gandhi, Mahatma, 58

grace, 4, 9
as gift to all, 26, 108
as greater than sin, 115
as transforming suffering, 76

hierarchy, *see also* Christians and the church
ambivalence of, 49, 53
and resistance to change, 45, 110
omissions of, 19, 51, 52, 54, 119
support from, around the world, 19, 75, 89
support from, in Brazil, 119, 120
visits from, 18, 19, 47, 62, 101, 102, 103, 119, 120

history
definition of, in relation to theology, 32, 95
God's presence in, 28, 70, 79, 88, 117, 124
present, as link between past and future, 95
as laid hold of by prophets, 25

holiness, as an ordinary condition, 28

Holy Spirit, 1, 5, 72, 90, 123
and Christian life, 14, 85, 101, 107, 112

hope, 16, 28, 71, 113

ideals, power of, 19

idolatry, of things in themselves, 61

impotence
feelings of, in prison, 17, 58, 80
in society, 118

injustice
Christian fight against, 6, 58
in world movements, 95

interrogations by police, 9, 66

Jesus, *see* Christ

joy, 1, 5, 80
of children, 27

kenosis, 52, 70, 79

kidnappings, reaction in prison to, 22, 84

King, Dr. Martin Luther, Jr., 58

kingdom of God, 3, 28, 32, 38, 40, 53, 70, 78, 81, 95, 104, 115

koinonia, 23

law, Christians and, 14

liberation, *see* freedom

love, meaning of, 104, 106, 112, 124

Marxism, listening to the message of, 26, 108

materialism, the concrete praxis of a consumer society, 68, 115, 118

metanoia, 23, 52, 56, 68, 114, 122

Nazism, comparison of Brazil's situation with, 16, 18, 51, 53, 54, 96, 119

nonbelievers
 author's concern for, 18
 holiness of, 9

noosphere, 25

novitiate, as critical experience, 67, 97

obedience, meaning of, 104

political prisoners
 as different from ordinary offenders, 99, 111, 114
 sufferings in families of, 34, 58, 119
 switching to support regime, 49
 treatment of, 13, 16, 19, 22, 120

poverty
 absence in church of, 55, 112, 117
 as means of union with Christ, 79, 97, 123
 meaning of vow of, 104

praxis
 as key to human life and history, 38, 56, 99, 123, 124
 renewal of Christian, 28, 38, 68, 70, 117, 122

priesthood
 and celibacy, *see* celibacy
 charisms of service and self-sacrifice in, 110
 flaws in priestly training and religious life, 38, 69, 79, 81, 90, 110
 as riding in all different directions, 68
 those leaving, 81

prison
 as theological experience, 13, 23, 25, 47, 71, 85, 107, 111, 113, 122
 degrading conditions of, 10, 13, 31, 48, 71, 72, 80, 85, 91, 98, 99, 114, 121
 experience of, summarized, 7, 122
 liturgical celebration in, 86, 103, 110, 122
 routine, activities, and opportunities in, 3, 6, 7, 8, 9, 11, 13, 14, 17, 18, 20,
  21, 22, 25, 33, 35, 37, 46, 48, 53, 58, 59, 60, 71, 72, 73, 77, 80, 83, 85, 86, 91,
  92, 93, 98, 99, 111, 114, 120, 121
 suspicions in, 13, 114
 tortures in, 13, 16, 19, 114, 120

rage, feelings of, in prison, 16, 17, 114

240

religious life
  author's novitiate experience in, 67
  bourgeois outlook in, 90, 115
  eventual demise of institutionalized, 81
  failure of personalization in, 111
  meaning of, 104
  passivity in, 69, 90
  renewal in, 68

religions, finding God in other, 42, 117

sacrament
  Christian as, in the world, 12
  prison as, 79

secularization, meaning of, for Christians, 28

social sciences, as attempts to understand ourselves, 25, 56, 110, 122

spirituality, definition of, 124

sports, paganism of, 61

suffering, intimating the presence of God, 23, 71, 75, 76, 78, 89, 96, 113, 114, 120, 121

television, negative influence of, 64, 66

theology, definition and perspectives of, 124

United States
  aid, 40
  author's view of, 25, 118
  imperialism, 54, 56, 95, 105, 124

values, shaken to the foundation, 115

vocation, of human beings, 23, 124

vows, meaning of religious, 104

waiting, in prison, 17, 48, 93

West
  distorted values of social order in, 64, 115
  growing up in values of, 118
  obsession with sex in, 118
  present social order wrongly identified with Christianity in, 45
  primitive moral and spiritual evolution of, 15
  reification in, 61

wisdom of men and folly of God, 7, 14, 116, 123

women, degradation of, 118

world, saved and loved by God, 115

yoga, practice of, in prison, 35

youth, expecting a more just world, 15, 66